Teen.

real teens

Diary of a
Junior Year

volume 2

W9-AKV-847

SCHOLASTIC INC.
New York Toronto London Auckland Sydney
Mexico City New Delhi Hong Kong

ISBN 0-439-08409-1

Distributed under license from
The Petersen Publishing Company, L.L.C.
Copyright © 1999 The Petersen Publishing
Company, L.L.C. All rights reserved.
Published by Scholastic Inc.

 Produced by 17th Street Productions,
a Division of Daniel Weiss Associates, Inc.
33 West 17th Street, New York, NY 10011

 Teen is a trademark of Petersen
Publishing Company, L.L.C.

SCHOLASTIC and associated logos are trademarks and/or
registered trademarks of Scholastic Inc.

12 11 10 9 8 7 6 5 4 3 2 1   9/9 0 1 2 3 4/0

Printed in the U.S.A.   01
First Scholastic Printing, October 1999

Special Thanks to Laura Dower

Diary of a Junior Year

volume 2

The diaries you are about to read are

real. Names, places, and other details

have been changed to protect the

teens involved. But what they have

to say all really happened.

Marybeth Miller:

I'm a wiseass. I can make just about anyone smile, even if they're feeling down in the dumps, and that's really important 2 me. Some days I consider myself fatter than others, but what are you gonna do, right? I run track and play basketball and keep on—so it's no big deal. Mostly I love just hanging out with my friends. Mom, Dad, and my brother and sister r cool 2, I guess. I mean, we don't _always_ get along, but I pull thru. I don't think I would want anything else.

    <u>LIKES:</u> My yellow Polo shirt

    <u>DISLIKES:</u> People who can't take a joke

Billy Shim:

I'm an outgoing, crazy guy, but I have mixed feelings about it. I'm smart and get good grades, but I know that's not good enough so I need something that stands out like sports, sports, sports! The scene with my parents is totally up/down. We have great moments, but we have arguments too—like good grades = heaven and bad grades = hell. But my older brother Lee, who's playing football at college right now, he's always there for me. Lee is the nicest guy you could ever meet. I think things would be easier if I were more like him.

LIKES: Sports, sports, sports (esp. lacrosse in spring)

DISLIKES: Stupid, clingy chicks

Teresa Falcone:

There is much more going on in my mind than the eye can see . . . I love writing, reading, dancing, singing, acting, playing field hockey, listening to all kinds of music, and most of all being with my friends and family. I know I'm smart and get really good grades, but I have this problem, which is everyone sees me as this airhead. I hate that! Sometimes I can be sooooo insecure! My parents are divorced, so I live with my mom and my older brother Vincent, even though we don't get along ever. My dad lives a town away, so I see him a lot.

<u>LIKES</u>: Romance books and anything else romantic!

<u>DISLIKES</u>: Not being taken seriously!

Jake Barosso.

Ladies think I'm cute, but only sometimes. I'm shy, but I love to dance and I'm always on the go. I love raving, riding a Jet Ski, playing pool, and fixing up my new car. My dad is really really sick, so things are terrible at home right now, but I try to help out as much as I can. We're always arguing about the stupidest things. I wish it didn't have to be like this. I like to make Mom + sis laugh whenever I can. I'm funny too.

<u>LIKES</u>: My car!!!

<u>DISLIKES</u>: Being sick + people who are assholes (a tie)

Katie Carson:

I am involved in Community Club and student council, on the tennis team, and a peer ministry leader of my church, among other things. To fit it all into one word, I am well-rounded. My schedule is nuts, but I handle stress with my sense of humor. I have important long-term goals for myself. Sometimes my friends tell me I am naive about things, but I really do believe I have the ability to get along with <u>everyone</u>. The most important thing to me is family — we're very close and share a special bond. I can tell my mom everything.

<u>LIKES</u>: Musical theater, travel, good grades, Brad

<u>DISLIKES</u>: People who don't have any goals

Edward Baxter:

This is me. I'm all the characteristics associated with this picture. I love listening to music, watching TV, and playing Nintendo. I'm a yearbook editor, sometimes I run track and I'm in Community Club, even though I'm starting to hate it, and I mean REALLY HATE IT. I'm also a bad speller, but for the most part I do well in school. As far as parents go, mine

are like big kids. My dad is a real comedian and my mom is
stupid funny, like me. My older brother Jerry is away at college.
    <u>LIKES</u>: Coconut my dog
    <u>DISLIKES</u>: People who never call you back, especially
when you beep them

<u>Emma West</u>:
   I think I'm totally trustworthy, kind,
and respectful, but if someone starts
talking about me behind my back I feel a
lot different and I get upset. At school
I'm ice-hockey manager and I'm in
community club and student council. I
love hanging out but I usually don't make
any plans until like the last minute,
usually with marybeth. The most important
thing is that my friends mean the world
to me. my parents are cool too. They're
always running around doing a million
different things and my little brother
Ronnie thinks he runs the house. my
sister Lynn and I have to babysit for nim

WhoWeAre WhoWeAre

a lot, which can be a drag but whatever.
<u>LIKES</u>: Having a boyfriend
<u>DISLIKES</u>: Being left out

Kevin MoRAn:
I'm All this. SMART, funny, hyper,
And I don't know whAt else kind of
guy. I kindA go from one thing to
Another like wAve running, clubbing,
swimming, mAinly Any sport—And mostly
just chilling with my friends. Still,
I get bored All the time. My
fAmily, they're loud, And DAd hAs
been mARRied 2x so we hAve A lottA
freAkin people here to deAl with
And we Argue like ALL THE TIME
but thAt's cool I guess cuz I
reAlly do love them All. I wAs
reAlly close to my sis LenA, but she
died like 8 yeARs Ago when I wAs 8,
which still mAkes me mAd.
<u>LIKES</u>: DRessing And doing stuff
exActly As I wAnt it And no one
cAn tell me Anything else
<u>DISLIKES</u>: My bRother Neil no
doubt!

Baxter

October 30

Today I wanted to go to the girls' soccer game but no one could give me a ride. And things with Megan aren't too good. She keeps blowing me off and hardly talks to me in school. I think I'm going to beep her again. I wonder what she's doing for Halloween?

marybeth

October 30th

Well, it's Friday, mischief night, and guess where I am? Babysitting. Fun, huh? Well, B4 I got here tonite I went to the girls' county soccer game and I saw that guy Rick Wright—and WE HOOKED ↑ AGAIN which was fun . . . but I just don't want anything right now with relationships. Really I don't.

You know the saying "No matter where you go, there you are"? That's me right now—feeling a little stuck like I just don't know WHAT I want. Oh, well. Gotta wait 4 these peeps to get home. Later.

Kevin

10/31

Today is Halloween and my car is like *finally* painted—YES! It looks soooo awesome in jet black w/purple and blue trim & I'm really happy I can't wait to drive all over the place and show everyone. I'm going to a Halloween party at Manny's tonight and I wish I could say the party was gonna rock but I know already it's not gonna be great AT ALL. Already this Halloween is DULL. It's the first time I haven't dressed up. I'm disappointed. Really my car is the best thing happening these days. I just *CAN'T STOP THINKING* about when I drove Adina home from her sister's party last night and we just sat in it and kissed forever. I think Adina and my car are like the best things that have ever happened to me.

Jake

October 31

Yesterday I went to the girls' state soccer game. Me and Kevin were late but we did make it. We lost, so going there was a total waste of time. Tonight our buddy Manny had a Halloween party. I just got back and I thought it was fun but no one else did. We drank a little because they spiked the

9

punch with vodka. Later on we left and went over to our friend May's house and shot pool and chilled out. Kevin got his car painted and it looks awesome. I am a little jealous because I love the paint job and how it looks. I can't wait until I get my license. 319 days to go. Ha ha.

Teresa

Oct 31 (1:30 a.m.)

Dear Diary,

Everyone has a license or a car except me, I swear! Why do I have to be the baby of the junior class? It can be such a drag getting around to parties and stuff. Anyway, technically Halloween's over now, but I had sooooo much fun today! I couldn't think of a really good costume so I just went trick or treating as a field-hockey player. I only did it for like 2 hours, but that was enough. I got sooooo much good candy. And since I went with my friends we could trade candy like a bunch of 2-year-olds. Basically I got whatever I wanted. I remember Halloween in third grade—I was dressed like a blue & silver mermaid! I remember wearing fishnets (ha ha), a silver leotard w/scales made from construction paper, a blond curly wig, and even egg cups for my chest! It was soooo funny. Imagine if I dressed like that *now*?

After trick or treating, I went over to my friend's

party and I was kinda mad because he told me no one was dressing up and I wanted to. That's what makes Halloween fun! I didn't really know a lot of the people there so I just sat around with Kevin and Adina and Jake and our other friend Mick Lazlo and acted really loud. Everyone was drinking (someone put something in the punch!) but none of us wanted to drink up, so we left at like 10 and went to some other girl's house and stayed out till like 1. And now I'm sleepy, oh well. More later.

Billy

10-31

Halloween today but who cares. I'm tired. Nothing has changed lately. All week I come home at 7 from football practice and do homework for like 3 or 4 hours. And then there are my football games. It's like today's game I woke up at 8:30 a.m. and ate breakfast with the team at 9:30. Then the anxiety kept building so we were mocking each other to take our mind off it. At 11:15 the warm-up started and I felt a little different. I can't explain it. I was thinking—would we really win? The game was at 1:00 and right before I walked out on the field I was so tense. I enjoy the games and the highs I get when I hit someone but today I wasn't so focused on that. I think the whole thing with Blair D. has me down. I don't care. I don't care about stupid Halloween.

P.S. We lost the game.

Katie

November 1
@ 12:04 A.M.

Today it felt so weird not to go trick or treating. I actually had planned to go as a ladybug, because I thought I would look really cute, but I couldn't find a costume that worked. I was at the mall with Gwen for almost three hours too. I was distraught! But Gwen and I bonded and that was nice. Since tennis ended, we have been trying to make more of an effort to see each other.

Actually, I had a pretty relaxing weekend, *FOR ONCE!* Last night for Halloween I had a bunch of people over including Gwen, Baxter, and of course Brad and his friend Tim. I invited Sherelle, Marybeth, and Emma and they were supposed to come but *that's* another story in itself. It seems like they always have *other* plans. I specifically asked Emma to let me know if she was going to miss it, but she didn't even call me. I just don't understand why.

p.s. I almost forgot! Today my dad called to reconfirm all our hotels and plane and *everything* for California! Later in November, we're going on a special trip since we have this short school break. It's going to be me, Mom, Dad, Patti, Paul, and lots of my cousins, *plus* Kevin and his family are going too, and he's bringing Jake. It should be so much fun to go see Disneyland and Knott's Berry Farm and all that stuff. Hooray!

Emma

11/1, 8:51 PM

Well my Halloween really sucked. I seriously did nothing last night. Yesterday afternoon was ok, I went to the football game with my cousin Barb again since she only lives a town away. Devin (that cool guy who gave me his football jersey) was playing and that stupid sophomore Alexis was there again. Like, she is the *LAST* person I wanted to see! The weird part is she said she was sorry and she didn't like Devin anymore and he was all mine. As if I really would want to go out with *HIM*! Whatever. I know she still wants him. She is just lying because she's scared of me. Anyway, later on I got home and talked to Marybeth and Sherelle and we agreed that we would hang out together for Halloween. Katie had asked us to her place too, but I wasn't really into that. So I took a shower and like 10 minutes later Marybeth calls back and says some kid was having a drinking party and we should all go. She knew I couldn't go because my other cousin might be there and he would *definitely* rat me out. I was really pissed because we were ALL supposed to hang out. Whatever. Lucky for me that party ended up canceled at the last minute and they called me at like 8:08 and said they would be here in 10 minutes so I should still get ready. I was psyched that we were going to hang out. But then it was like 9:00 and they still were not here so I was upset. And when they finally did arrive, we went by this park and I couldn't believe it because everyone there was *DRINKING*! I told Sherelle I would not get in a car with Bobby who was also drinking but she just ignored me. Later on she was pissed too though because Bobby was even ignoring *HER* just to drink beer. So what happened was me, Marybeth, Sherelle, and this kid Rick Wright left and went to go get some food. I was so hungry for some reason. We drove by a 7-Eleven and found Wright's other friends too, which was cool, although we ended up standing in the parking lot there for like an hour and I was freezing my butt off. I guess Halloween could have been better but whatever. Cliff wanted me to go with him to some party but I felt too stupid. Plus I wasn't really invited.

xoxoxoxox Emma

Marybeth

November 1st

So my Halloween was okay I guess. Yesterday I woke up @ 9:30, took a shower, and went to the football game. Later on Sherelle, Bobby, Wright, and I headed to this drinking party but it got canceled, so we went to this place Mountain View instead and just shot the shit and hit the swings. Nothing much. Then we got Em and some of us went to the Silverado and 7-Eleven. Oh yeah, and I wore furry bunny ears and I looked kinda cute. Wright kept asking me to hop around.

Today a group of us went over to the driving range in town and went to the mall. I was pigging out on jelly beans. *MY BAD*—but I love them! I'm reading the Cliffs Notes for *Billy Budd*. I have a lot of homework that I should be doing but I don't want to. My mom is on my back about that.

Baxter

November 1

Today we went over to my grandparents' house and had macaroni and meatballs. My gram cooks such *GREAT* food! Actually, this whole weekend was a family weekend. Friday we went to my dad's old house about an hour away to eat with his favorite uncle and aunt. Dad wanted to go see them because my great-uncle just had his hip replaced and he can't really get around. Since my dad's mom got sick when he was just a kid, he went to live with my uncle and my aunt so they were like his suragate parents, I guess. I think I spelled that wrong. Anyway, they're both really nice but I can't imagine how my dad survived living there. I can't imagine what it would be like without my mom.

Katie

November 2
@ 7:11 P.M.

Just got off the phone with Em who says she's sorry about the Halloween thing and not calling to let me know. She said she just forgot, but I don't know whether to believe her so I'll just forget about it.

I think I'm going to be bored to tears until the school musical starts in December. And I have to watch my weight more now that tennis is finished for the year! PLUS, I have to think of the perfect gift for Brad who was so cute this weekend when he bought me this Edwin McCain CD I wanted. I'm actually kind of sick of him buying me stuff since I am not creative enough to do it back to him, but now I have to get him *SOMETHING*. I have too many errands to do! When will I ever get it all done?

Baxter

November 2

Today sucked. I have three labs to do for AP chemistry and physics in which I don't know what the hell is going on. Mr. MacTaggart is so confusing. But I did get 100 on my math, so that's good. Meanwhile Miss Shapiro, aka *THE COW* from Community Club, pissed me off once again. First of all, she doesn't talk *to* me, she always talks behind my back. Then she says my announcements are bad and my articles are too short all of a sudden even though they were just fine for the last 4 editions. I think I hate her. Anyway I just talked to Marybeth and she's going to call me back. I think I will try beeping Megan too. Let me go desperately wait for her call! Please call!

Marybeth

November 3rd

Wow was today a long day. I had to write a report

on *Billy Budd* and that took a while. I didn't even go to track practice b/c of the report. I am NOT in a good mood, but I am not PMS-ing or anything. I'm not mad at anyone, either. Why am I so upset? Oh well. Maybe tomorrow will be a little better. I hope so. I got this note from Sherelle in class today when she was trying to cheer me up. She wanted to know if I had hooked up with Mr. Wright (ha ha, that's what she calls Rick as a joke). She makes me laugh.

I'm trying to decide if I should hang out with her & the guys from across town later. Sher has a field hockey game but after that we can go. She says they wanna see me. I guess I'd be stupid to pass that up.

Kevin

11/3

Okay, this last week sucked *A LOT*. It all started w/Halloween. I didn't dress up like I said I would yeah yeah and now I really wish I had—well I'll live. And now this week sucks so much too I am happy just to *STAY AWAKE IN CLASS*. I dunno why I am so tired. I have been on the phone with Adina a lot so maybe I just need more sleep!!! Hey Jake just passed me this stupid note in class about Claudia. She's in this class too, sitting up at the front (we're in the back). He's obsessed. I've been thinking that maybe Teresa and Jake should hook up again, like it would do him a lotta good. But of course Teresa will not go for it unless she's sure he's over Claudia so forget that. Hopefully they will both be happy no matter what happens. Maybe I should just keep out of it . . . but I just want to help if I can help. That's just the way I am. Oh yeah, Dad *FINALLY* got the tickets for Disneyland like I couldn't believe that he waited until the absolute last minute! I was scared like maybe we wouldn't be able to go or something. Anyway, it's cool now & Jake is coming w/us so that should cheer him up a lot.

A Little Help From My Friends

Jake:

My friends help me the most just by chilling. They know how to crack me up.

Katie:

All my friends have different styles and interests and the diversity helps make me a better person. I've become a lot more accepting lately. It's never my place to talk negatively about any of my friends.

Billy:

The guys on the football team are one kind of friend and guys like Kevin or Bax are another type. I do different stuff to help different friends. Depends on who I'm with.

Marybeth:

A friend helps me by being positive. I can't stand people who r negative b/c it drags me down.

A Little Help From My Friends

Kevin:

   I think friends have a TOTAL responsibility to be there for one another like how I feel about Jake most of the time needing my support w/his dad, and how I felt last year when I knew Katie needed support when she was in that relationship w/that asshole, and how I feel when anyone needs me to listen to them if their b/f or g/f is cheating, or to defend them, or anything I will be there rain or shine

Emma:

   True friends stay loyal no matter what else is going on. That's the rule. And friends help you out when you need it, even if it conflicts with their social calendar.

A Little Help From My Friends

<u>Baxter:</u>

Friends help you by listening. I can ALWAYS count on Emma because I can tell her anything. Not only that but she keeps me informed on all the gossip and calls me when something is going on, unlike some other people I know.

<u>Teresa:</u>

I don't really have much faith in friendship these days, as much as I wish I did. I think it's overrated. No one could possibly be your friend for LIFE.

22

Teresa

Dear Diary,

I heard from my friend Jesse today, this guy I met at a hockey game a while ago. Anyway, he's really sweet and *HOT* and we really hit it off and hung out . . . so I guess you could say that him and me are together. We look really good as a couple. But actually, we're not *TECHNICALLY* "together" since I hooked up with Jake a couple of weeks ago at my Sweet 16. (I didn't want to write anything about that b/c I was a little embarrassed at first, but the truth is it was pretty cool.) To be perfectly honest, the thing w/Jake hasn't gone anywhere since that nite.

What am I supposed to do? I mean, if Jake ever wanted a real relationship with me I think I would be willing, but I *HAVE TO* accept the fact that he's still in love with Claudia. And with Jake out of the picture then Jesse and I should probably keep talking and maybe hook up to see if we have a romantic future together, right? Of course, I still think about Kevin sometimes too.

WHAT IS WRONG WITH ME?

I love Kevin *and* Jake and always have but I *HAVE TO* accept just being good friends with them. That's all. And I'm still getting to know Jesse so something could maybe still happen there. More later, I'm sure.

Billy

11-4

Today was awesome. I finally got my license and took Blair D. for a ride. She thought I was extremely cool and that's exactly the way I wanted it. She and I are starting to click. She says it's so cool that I have transport and now we can go places together. I know I'm going to go places without her too that's for sure. It's MY car.

Emma

11/4, 4:48 PM

Billy got his license today. I am so happy for him! And things have gotten pretty good with Cliff. Last night we talked for two hours and it went really well. I told him how people in school were talking about him and me going out and he laughed. I was like, "Why are you laughing?" He said he believed me. That's all. Whatever. I know there's another girl at JFK, Lainie, who likes him but he doesn't like her. Well, she's kind of BIG. Sometimes I think she's giving me dirty looks in the hallway. Other times I think she's trying to suck up to me. Like a little while ago when I was on the computer she IM'ed me and told me she liked my new haircut. I was shocked! So we talked a little bit and I was nice to her but I think she's kind of weird for doing that. Like if she's talking to me to be my friend, that's cool . . . but if she's just trying to get information about Cliff, that's another thing. She can go somewhere else! Like I've said before, I hate people who are two-faced and talk shit behind your back.

Marybeth

November 5th

Today was a little better than yesterday. Emma and Sherelle and I hung out at lunch. We haven't done that in a while. She's really into this Cliff guy. He's e-mailing her all the time. Or at least that's what she was saying. Anyway, I got a cool fortune cookie from dinner tonite:

> THE WORLD IS A GRAND COMEDY TO YOUR SENSE OF HUMOR.
> LUCKY NUMBERS: 1, 2, 3, 17, 27, 37

That describes me perfectly.

I took a chem quiz today that I thought was sorta hard but I'm not gonna think about it too much. Oh well.

My mommy said a little prayer to me this morning and I don't wanna forget it: *Step by step, prayer by prayer, the Lord will always get you there.* I think it's cute. But when she told me, it made me wanna call my dad at work for no reason. I just wanted to say hi and I love you. It was like a part of me felt like I wouldn't get another chance to do that. Is that weird? I think I need to make more of an effort to be good to my dad. Whenever I have a sinking feeling like that or have a dream, something happens. Makes me freak out a little. I think about how hard it's been for Jake & his dad and that would be so awful to deal with.

Jake

November 6

Today is another bad day, even for a Friday. I miss my dad.

It used to be so great when I was a kid. I remember when my brother, me, and my little sister would be playing basketball and Dad and Mom would come outside and try to play with us. My dad had this funny way of running and chasing the ball. I remember how he would stop to shoot it. And soccer too. He would always give us tips on how to kick and play and do all kinds of sports.

A few months before he was diagnosed I remember we were down by the beach and we challenged Dad to a lifting contest and my brother and I were making fun of him because he couldn't bench-press like us and he was having trouble. All of a sudden he was weaker than before. Then a little bit later was when the doctor told him he had Becker MD, this special kind of muscular dystrophy. I felt so bad about that.

Around that time we were also planning this party and Mom said we had to wait to hear what Dad's doctor had to say. If he said Dad was ok we could party and if not then everything was over. Of course then Dad came home and told me how sick he was and it was the *WORST DAY OF MY WHOLE LIFE*. He was on my bed hugging me and Mom was in the chair in the corner. He was crying, I was crying, and all I could do was hug him. It kills me that there is no cure for him. I feel this is a punishment for something we did wrong. What did I do wrong?

Katie

555-3271,
where Brad is

November 6
@ 11:15 P.M.

Right now I am waiting up in bed for Brad to call me. I beeped him 4 times and he hasn't called me. Wait. That may be him on the phone now.

No, it was his friend Tim who said Brad was just sleeping and to stop beeping! Yeah, right! He wanted to know if Brad could just call me back tomorrow. What is going on here? Tim says he's just tired but I don't believe him. There's no way Brad's asleep, I can tell. I got worried so Tim put Brad on the phone anyway. He was practically gone, meaning *DRUNK*. And that didn't bother me so much. What bothered me was that he *LIED* trying to say he was asleep when he was really drinking! He knows how I feel about that. He told me to just stop worrying but I can't deal. He said he loved me and he'd call me tonight and now I am so pissed! I mean, what if he was really sick or something? What am I supposed to do? I'd even consider calling his parents but he'd really be dead meat then if they found out he was drinking. Oh, good night already!

11:36 P.M.

Brad just called me again and he was *TOTALLY* drunk this time and he could barely talk! He practically hung up on me. But he said not to worry and his friends would take care of him. Well, I guess now that that's taken care of I should just relax and go to sleep.

Nov 6 (11:00 P.M.)

Dear Diary,

Everyone needs to *JUST RELAX*—including me! For whatever reason people were snapping at each other all day today. I took this history quiz and had to meet with my teacher after school and when we met I asked her how I did and she said, "You don't want to know." Well thanks a lot! What is she snapping at ME for? That got me sooooo upset because right now my average is like a low B to begin with and now it will be so much worse. Also, I took this awful math test and I already know for sure I got 1 out of 5 questions *WRONG*!!! What a day! And now it's late and I still have homework backed up. How am I going to get everything done and go on a date with Jesse this weekend? This sucks. I hope my horoscope for today is right, because I need some serious help!

Don't freak out about stuff happening around the 7th of this month. Just keep your real priorities in mind. Why not transfer your verbal gifts to the page? Poems, journals, and letters all have deeper meaning for you this month. Pull out a Bic and go for it.

I need to keep up with my poetry some more!

Katie

November 8
@ 7:43 P.M.

Just got off the phone with Brad (again) and I think (for good) we've cleared up what happened Friday when he was drunk. The truth is he overdrank and passed out on the floor for *TWO* hours. He called me yesterday to explain but I didn't really want to hear it so I didn't take his call. I said I was mad and I was. But I felt bad talking to him today. He was really upset about it all. He told me he was scared and I was terrified to hear him say that. I am just not used to this kind of behavior. I don't know how to react.

I know I have to accept it on some level. I mean, every guy drinks—Kevin, Jake, Billy. And Baxter doesn't really, but maybe he should. It's just a fact of life. A stage that they have to grow out of. And Brad has so many other assets, I can deal with this one flaw, right?

It's just that I want to feel safe around Brad *all the time*. Like when he holds me in his strong arms—I can't explain it—it's like nothing and no one can hurt me ever. And the drinking just makes me nervous sometimes. I'm still scared of being hurt again like I was with Robert but I guess that may never totally go away no matter who I date. I have to deal with certain things. Like I have this belief that when the fighting starts, the relationship is over, but that's not really true. For example, even if Brad calls me a "spoiled princess," we're still together. I get upset *OF COURSE* but we're still together. I guess it can work even through not so great times. I guess I have to wait and see.

p.s. I figured out my predicted grades for this marking period, based on my last tests. It's worse than I have ever done before, but not devastatingly bad, I guess. I'll do better next time. I have to try and bring them up by a month or so from now. The *best* surprises (not all my subjects are here):

Gym A+
AP History B (what a save, considering!)
Choristers A+
Advanced Chemistry B- (oh well, but at least I didn't FAIL)
Photog. A+ (I love this!!!)

Emma

11/9, 7:01 PM

I should be working right now, but I don't feel like it. My grades are good enuf! I am so psyched because the whole Cliff thing just keeps getting better and better. That big girl Lainie is still trying to be my friend but I am just ignoring her and I wish she would get out of my face already. Cliff is *MINE*! I saw him on Saturday and we got a chance to dance this weekend at some kid's Sweet 16. Lainie was there too so I hope she takes a hint! Anyway, the next day Cliff's friend Josh e-mailed me and said that Cliff wanted to ask me out! I was soooo shocked when I read it on the computer screen:

```
Cliff wants to ask you out.
Do you want to go?
```

31

I mean, me and Cliff have been talking on the phone for like 2 hours every night and I had *NO IDEA* this was gonna happen like this. In fact, maybe Josh is making it all up. But what if that is true? Then what?

Baxter

November 9

Megan never calls me back. Ever. I asked her about it in school this morning and she just changed the subject and laughed and told me she was busy.

So much is happening in school. I lost my temper today in history class when we had to pick topics for our debates. I got stuck with *pro*-affirmative action and I am morally against that so it made it impossible to support. *WHAT REALLY PISSED ME OFF* was that this kid Chris in class picked the subject of "animal testing" before I could. He knew that was what I wanted but he picked it anyway. I mean that sucks!! Here is a kid who votes for censorship so why didn't he pick that? I wished out loud that Chris would just go to hell. Of course everyone seemed pleased to see me cursing and getting so aggravated, which was a little strange. Except Chris, who yelled back. It was an ugly situation. I feel a little bad about it but he just pissed me off!!!

I'm going to go beep Megan for the last time

ever. If she does not call me back I will just live with my heart being broken forever and *that's that*.

p.s. gotta go study for three tests or else I'm screwed . . .

Katie

November 9
@ 8:00 P.M.

I've been noticing problems in my friends' families lately and the effects they're having on the kids. Like Baxter's parents are really pushing him hard lately. Way too hard. They want him to get into a good school and get a scholarship. His mom won't let him go anywhere or do anything until he's spent at least 3 or 4 hours on homework. I have known him all my life and it's having a *HUGE* effect on him. He was always upbeat before and now he's so pessimistic. Everyone has noticed it too. He's not accepting any of our jokes and talks about everyone behind their backs. I just called him a little while ago and reminded him of our Community Club meeting this week and he said he couldn't go because he has homework! That really is a drag because I can't carry his responsibilities in addition to my own. Baxter is one of my very best friends in the whole world but sometimes I get angry at him too.

What Pisses Me Off

Kevin:

I hAve A short fuse so like just About Anything cAn set me off. Either An Argument or just listening to people fight—sooo mAny different things. Sometimes it's freAky how pumped up I cAn get, like I'm A different person w/A dif. mind.

Katie:

I think getting angry is a waste of my time. I don't like how it feels to be upset, like being nauseous. And if other people are mad, I usually try to be the moderator.

Teresa:

I get soooooo mad if someone stabs me in the back. Like how I feel about my old friend since childhood, Wendy, who lives near me. She's my BFF and then suddenly she's never around. She completely

34

What Pisses Me Off

blows me off. It makes me feel like
nothing.

Billy:

I get mad when I don't do well on my schoolwork or when I mess up a play in a game. Losing makes me mad

Marybeth:

I think mostly I let stuff just roll off my back. Sometimes I guess I get a little pissed off, like if someone acts like a real jerk 2 me w/friends, I get mad 4 a little while. But I get over it real fast. It's just not worth it.

Jake:

I don't think it's fair that my dad has to be so sick. Mostly I am just feeling sad, but sometimes I think I could pound on someone I get so angry.

What Pisses Me Off

Emma:

A lot of stuff pisses me off a lot of the time like when people don't listen, when people talk awful shit about you and you find out about it, or when someone steals your b/f.

Baxter:

I get so angry if people question my thoughts or my beliefs, or start talking badly about my family or the way I was brought up or anything. I take that really personally. I can't stand it when people think they're so much better than you and the truth is they're the stupid idiots.

Kevin

I am so mad right now. I get angry pretty easily these days and I have a pretty short fuse. Um, I guess the main cause of my anger has to be my family. So many different things. First, my brother Neil. I hate him so much and we are *ALWAYS* fighting.

Then there's my mom who is very picky and extremely hard to live with it's like *no matter what I do it's NEVER good enough.* She rarely says thank you either and so these things spark a lot of our fights. But I just let it be as much as possible because the truth is that all parents and kids argue. And my dad and I only fight occasionally like when I'm in a bad mood. This morning was one of those times and I thought I made it perfectly clear to my dad that he shouldn't *MESS WITH ME.* And of course he did anyway. He was cracking some joke and I got all pissy and then he screamed about how I don't appreciate everything he does for me. It kinda exploded after that. He doesn't realize that I DO appreciate it. I do.

I am just so glad I have Adina so I can let go of everything once in a while. She is so great and listens to me. I could never get mad at her I don't think.

Billy

In the last few weeks, I've gotten a lot of letters from colleges in the mail. Mostly letters about football. I also took my PSATs. With all that *and* getting my license last week it seems like everything is really happening so fast. Blair D. and I are heating up these days too. She got me this great CD for my birthday (I'm listening to it right now). The thing is, we get along so great, so it's hard not to want her. We can talk for hours on the phone about anything at all. But I'm not sure I can deal with having a girlfriend right now. I have to focus on school and teams. Football and lacrosse will get me noticed for a good college I think, like it did for my brother Lee. Of course, he had better grades when he was a junior. He was #1 though which is maybe too much to live up to.

Jake

November 10

I think my grades are suffering a little because of what's going on at home. I tried to talk to my dad about it today but he was pretty tired. How can all this bad luck happen to one person? My dad came from Puerto Rico to raise us and he worked his ass off to give us anything we needed or wanted like a beautiful home and other stuff that most people only dream about. In fact, the other night I had this dream. In it, my mom and me were in the kitchen cooking and all of a sudden upstairs there was my dad and he was screaming because he could walk again. He could *WALK*! He just came up to us screaming and walking and I swear that was the greatest day of my whole life. After that we could start planning all the things we could do to make up for lost time.

But it was a dream.

p.s. We're leaving for California in two days. Kevin is so awesome for letting me go with his family.

Katie

November 10
@ 6:20 P.M.

Right now I am on a plane on my way to Disneyland and I am so excited I can't believe it. This great feeling actually started yesterday when I found out that I am getting an A+ in history—the one seemingly impossible feat! And I am the *ONLY ONE* getting such a high grade! *A PLUS!* I could've sworn I'd get a B+ but I guess I was wrong—thank goodness. Plus now I'm on my way to Anaheim, California, with my family. Hooray!

This morning I went to school and something *REALLY* strange happened. About 2 months ago I was in the guidance office and decided to apply for the honor of representing my high school at a conference for our state. About 20 people applied (I actually think Teresa did too) and today was when they called me and this other kid Carlos down to let us know that we were the finalists. Carlos is in the top five, and I bet our class ranks differ by only like a hundredth of a point, so I'd say we're *EVEN*! We'll be evaluated against each other by comparing our resumes and by having several different interviews. I just printed out a copy of my most recent resume from freshman, sophomore & junior years and I think it looks pretty good. It will mean *A LOT* to me if I get this position.

PROFILE OF STUDENT REPORTED ACTIVITIES

Name: Kathryn Diane Carson

School: John F. Kennedy High School

SCHOLASTIC DISTINCTIONS OR HONORS GRADE(S)

Science League Participant (Biology/Chemistry) 9, 10, 11

Spanish Excellence Award 9

Spanish Honors Society 10, 11

National Honor Society 11

2nd Place, Kids for Political Freedoms Contest 10

Community Club—Distinguished Secretary 10

National Student Leadership Conference 10

Community Service Award 10

ATHLETIC DISTINCTIONS OR HONORS GRADE(S)

Varsity Tennis 9, 10, 11

Varsity Track 9, 10

Awards: 3rd Place County Championships, 2nd Team 10

Conference, and Mangrove Tennis Club Doubles Champion 10

SCHOOL ACTIVITIES GRADE(S)

Community Club 9, 10, 11

Outstanding Member, Secretary, and President

Yearbook 9, 10

Photographer and Sophomore Editor

Student Government 9, 10, 11

Liaison to Board of Education; Vice President

Club Espanol

Choir Advanced Madrigals (Featured Soloist) 9

Drama Club 10, 11

Guys and Dolls (Dancer/Chorus); *The Women* (Lead Role)

Newspaper *Impact*, Features Editor 9, 10

Homecoming Co-chairperson 10

Semiformal Co-chairperson 10

COMMUNITY ACTIVITIES

Hospital Volunteer (150+ hours); Homeless Shelter Volunteer; Peer Minister; Habitat for Humanity; Little Miss Beauty Pageant; Blood Drive; Senior Center; UNICEF

SUMMER AND OTHER ACTIVITIES

State University Junior Biologists Program; foreign travel; tap dancing

Emma

What am I doing with my life? I am so sick of wasting my time worrying about Sherelle and Marybeth. All day at school I was talking with them about going out and now I am in the worst mood because they ditched me. The plan was that we were going to go out after this soccer game. So afterwards, Marybeth says that wait a minute plans had changed and now Sherelle and Bobby were going to go eat together first since it was their one-month anniversary. And since they were going to eat, now Marybeth wanted to go eat too, but not with me . . . with that kid Rick Wright. Whatever. That leaves me out for a while. But they still said we could all hook up later. So I borrowed my sister's beeper and told them to let me know when they were ready to go. They never beeped me. And I am sure that right now the two of them are dreaming up some excuse to tell me about why they ended up blowing me off. The truth is *I REALLY DON'T GIVE A SHIT*! I am so tired of the two of them ditching me for Bobby and Rick. And my sister got *PLENTY* of beeps so I know the beeper works just fine. And this is *NOT* the first time this has happened. Ever since Sherelle and Marybeth have been hanging around this particular group of girls who drink and have sex, everything is changed. Everyone calls them "The Mix" because that's what these girls always do, they mix it up with guys who are older and all that. It sucks. I mean, *EXCUSE ME* for not being into that and not having a boyfriend who is on the football team! Marybeth keeps telling me she doesn't like this Wright kid but I say she's leading him on . . . big time. She is a liar. This weekend we're going away on a church retreat and I know she will be all nice to me and talk about Sherelle like nothing ever happened or like nothing is the matter. Whatever. I feel like going off on her when she does this. If she's so sorry and doesn't want me to feel left out then why does she always hang out with Sherelle? I dunno. I am sure one of them if not both of them will call me before I go to bed tonite and will ask me what's up. I have decided that when they DO start making up those excuses, then I will just act like I don't care. And I don't. Or at least I won't. The truth is that they just forgot about me or they just don't want to be around me. I wish I could stay mad at them for once. It's just that I'm afraid to. I don't want to lose my two best friends.

xoxoxoxox Emma

Marybeth

November 11th
Last night I went drinking. It wasn't very cool though. I had like 3 shots of J.D. I don't even like

Jack Daniels. It was so funny though b/c my bf Sherelle was with me. She had like 6 shots. And she is still puking today. I'm glad that wasn't me.

Em was supposed to hang out with us but I dunno what happened. Actually that's good b/c of the whole drinking thing, I guess. I mean she's so worried about getting caught. She's always been like that. In 6th grade I hated her. She seemed real bitchy. 5 years later I've concluded that she is bitchy, just not all the time. A lot of people think she's annoying and I know she has her moments, but who doesn't? I'd still die 4 her. Oh and b/t/w— My brother Mitch is in the next room right now and he's farting. He's a pistol.

Teresa

Nov 11 (1:00 p.m.)

Dear Diary,

Trouble in paradise. Gina and I are upset w/our other friend Stephanie because she has been spending so much time with her boyfriend that we *never* see her. She talks about him *all* the time, she's always w/him, and that's all she cares about. But when me and Gina told her how we felt about this, she got kinda mad. To me, that is really immature because it is a problem and we have every right to discuss it! Tonight I'm supposed to go sleep over at Stephanie's and I think we're gonna discuss everything all over again. I hope so. I mean, I know everything will turn out ok in the end, but we have so much to work out first. We need to clear things up. My belief is that if friends can't make time for each other, then there is no real friendship to begin with. They should come first and foremost over everything. People who choose their boyfriends over their friends have some MAJOR problems . . . because I know *boyfriends come and go but best friends stay forever.* I will never forget this.

p.s. I asked Marybeth what she thought about the whole scene and she thinks Gina and I should just be honest even if Stephanie doesn't want to hear the truth. Thank God for Marybeth! She is such a good friend to me, I don't think she realizes how much.

Billy

11-11

Blair D. and I are still spending a lot of time together, even though I am not sure what I want to do about it. I feel kind of pressured all around me these days. I'm not sure how to explain it, it's just there. Sometimes it's football or sports and then other times I feel like I should be dating a hotter girl than I am. Mostly it has to do with schoolwork.

I definitely feel pressured to do everything at school because I am expected to. I have to go to a great college. In my parent's eyes, good grades and activities are the keys to getting in. Right now I'm 19/282 kids so I am in the top of our class. Plus I am singing again and I'm starting in 2 varsity letter sports, blah, blah, blah. So I think I'm doing the right stuff but the pressures are getting to me. The only thing I really love is lacrosse, which doesn't start until the spring. Why can't I just stop thinking so much about all this stuff?

Marybeth

November 12th

All day I have been in a sort of "to myself" mood. I don't know why. I have done so much thinking that I'm tired. All afternoon I babysat but that wasn't too bad because I made $22.00. Tonight I'm off to a retreat meeting—my last one. Tomorrow the retreat starts and I'll be home sometime on Sunday. I'm glad I already finished the 100 pages I have to read for English. It's total craziness how tired I feel. Maybe I'll take a nap. I just need some quiet time alone.

When I Wanna Be Alone

<u>Kevin:</u>
in the summer i just go hang out by the swings at the beach and just listen to the water and think and no one is there to get in my face

<u>Katie:</u>
There's a small room in JFK where I go when school gets too overwhelming. It used to be a music room or something like that so it's soundproofed and really quiet.

<u>Teresa:</u>
I stay in my room with the music blasting! I can lose myself in my music.

<u>Billy:</u>
I drive around in my car with the radio on.

<u>Marybeth:</u>
I usually like to be with other peeps, but sometimes I like to go 4 a long run. . . .

47

When I Wanna Be Alone

Jake:
  I go to the beach.

Emma:
  I love to shut the door and be in my room. It is my own private space and no one can bother me.

Baxter:
  I hate to be alone!!!

Emma

11/12, 4:30 PM

I can't get anything done today. I have a ton of homework but I'm just sitting here. I feel wiped out for some reason. I didn't really talk to Sherelle or Marybeth at school today. Maybe that's it. I feel really weird because they have all these inside jokes between them and I am just left standing there looking stupid. Whatever. I am trying to get over this situation but I can't seem to get the two of them out of my head. They always seem to give me this attitude!

I should really try to do my English reading but I can't. I think I'll watch *Forgive or Forget* or something else on TV. Maybe I'll go call Baxter. Maybe I'll go online.

Baxter

November 12

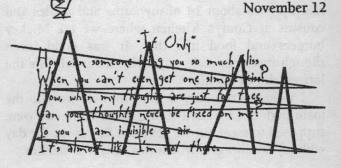

"If Only"

How can someone bring you so much bliss?
When you can't even get one simple kiss?
How, when my thoughts are just for thee,
Can your thoughts never be fixed on me?
To you I am invisible as air.
It's almost like I'm not there.

49

If only you knew the meals I hadn't eaten
If only you knew how hard my heart was beating
How very very much that I love you
If only you knew, if only you knew.

tHIS SUCKS!

Katie

November 12
@ 11:00 P.M.

So we're in sunny California now and this is the most *BEAUTIFUL* place I could ever have imagined. Right now I am curled up on this super cushy sofa inside the lobby of the Disneyland Hotel and so far everything has gone smoothly. Kevin and Jake are coming tomorrow with Kevin's family, so it should be *GREAT*! Yesterday Mom, Dad, Patti, Paul, and I met up with about 14 of my aunts and uncles and cousins at Goofy's Kitchen where we ate Mickey burgers and food like that. It was good, even though that's not really my style. Today felt like the longest day of my life!

I woke up this a.m. at 6:30, and we went to the main park but I missed seeing Kevin there (we were supposed to meet but we got lost). So I spent the day with my family again which was okay. We had fun.

We spent a lot of time in Tomorrowland (it's all new now) and later we got to see this show called "Fantasmic" or something like that. It was an unbelievable light and laser spectacle with these Disney villains! I am so lucky!

But the best part was what happened later in the afternoon. I couldn't believe it! When we were eating lunch at this fast-food place inside Frontierland, I saw a friend of mine from like 10 years ago! Well, from 7th grade anyway. Back then she moved away from our town and school. Her name is Leigh and we had tried to stay in touch like pen pals but lost track a summer ago. Anyway, she looked so great! When I saw her I couldn't stop jumping up and down like a part of me inside had been rejuvenated.

The only embarrassing thing today was at dinnertime, at this totally crazy restaurant in the hotel. Our waiter started to pick on me for no reason. Well, he was trying to be funny. He overheard me making some comment and teasing my mom so he made me ride this wooden horse around the lobby and I had to scream, "I love and worship my amazing mother." It was pretty silly but I laughed.

p.s. This has to stop! I was just hit on by like the 5th guy tonight. It's so frustrating! (It does make me feel good, but they're all dorks and I do have a boyfriend.)

11/13

We got here to Cali two days ago and have been going places and doing shit *NONSTOP* ever since. The first night we got here I was pretty tired after the flight and all. It was like 10:30 by the time we even got to our hotel so we just unpacked and went to bed. Then yesterday we all went to the park: me, my dad and mom and my little sister and Jake (his parents didn't come for obvious reasons). We didn't do a lot. Really we just went on random rides and stuff like that. We also spent a bunch of time swimming at our hotel and I went to this shopping arcade for a minute and I saw a really cute locket and I got it for Adina just for the hell of it. Plus we walked around Toontown or whatever it's called and I took a lot of pictures. Later that night we went over to the Disneyland Hotel where Katie's family is staying and we went looking for them and found out they were in the restaurant. It was so weird because when we walked in there was some stupid ass girl riding around on a wooden horse and me and Jake were making fun of her. Then we found out it was Katie—but she was so far away we couldn't see her. My bad! Anyway, today is pretty much the same only tonight Adina is coming here to join us and that's cool. I'm gonna go with her to this "Fantasy in the Sky" fireworks show they're advertising. It sounds like it might be really good w/lasers and music. Plus from Katie's hotel we can ride a monorail right into the park.

Jake

I can't believe I am really in California especially after everything that has been going on at home. I was so ready for this trip. I need time away from girls and everything else so I can just have some fun. The only bad part is that when we left for the airport, *I was so worried* about my dad. I didn't want to leave him and right before I left he had to go into the hospital. He went in for some more tests, which sucked. He was getting a test *exactly at the same moment* that I was getting on a plane! I was worried, just praying and praying. But anyway, Mom told me everything would be ok so I'm here with Kevin and his family. We've been going to every attraction at Disney and today Knott's Berry Farm and we are probably going to the San Diego Zoo later on. It's the greatest week I've had ever. We are doing so much and walking so much. We went nuts and took great pictures today and I ate so much Pizza Hut because there's one up the street from the hotel. I went swimming too, which was good since I am on the swim team at school now. Katie's hotel has this phat rooftop swimming pool.

Teresa

Nov 13 (9:45 p.m.)

Dear Diary,

Well, another week at school is over and Gina, Stephanie, and I *STILL* haven't discussed the whole Stephanie/boyfriend/friend thing. But we definitely will this weekend. I know we will. Gina and I made a pact. Anyway, I'm not really thinking about that so much right now because I just talked to this guy I like named Zach. He graduated last year from JFK with my brother. I got his screen name and then we met up in a chat room on AOL and after a while he asked for my phone number. Well, I gave it to him and then we talked in person and it was soooooo great! (I was sooooo surprised.) I can't wait to see him on a real date, if that happens. Actually, it's kinda weird because this guy Zach and Jake are friends and since I hooked up with Jake a few weeks ago, it seems a little strange. But I'll wait to see what happens with Jake and Claudia and then I'll figure out what's going on with Zach.

Katie

Jake is so funny! Today we were at Knott's Berry Farm and he and I had an ice fight at one of the refreshment stands. He whipped a chunk of ice at me and gave me this huge black and blue welt! Then Kevin and Jake made me stand on line for like 2 hours (maybe I am exaggerating a little) just to ride this *HUGE* wooden roller coaster called the Supreme Scream. It was out of control! We were all crammed together in this long line waiting and then two of them started clapping and making lewd comments and being obnoxious in general. It was actually really funny!

Later on I met up with my family and went back to Disneyland (my favorite place!) and I loved it because the lines there had gotten so much shorter and we could walk right into every single ride and exhibit. We rode on the Indiana Jones one twice! There is just something so magical about that place. It's the whole castle bit and everything—I can't explain the feeling that I get when I am there. It's like my soul lets go of everything serious in life and I am 5 years old again!

It's weird to think about getting older. When we were hanging out waiting for a Country Bear show to start this afternoon, I noticed this girl sitting in front of me and she was about my age. She was a pretty girl who kind of reminded me of myself in that she looked really naive and innocent. She was with her two younger sisters, her parents, and her boyfriend, and it just seemed so familiar. I was thinking about how lucky she was and I was missing Brad, and then all of a sudden the girl stood up and I saw the most horrifying sight. She was pregnant. How horrible it was to see a girl my age sitting there with her life ruined by one mistake! I started thinking what if she was top in her class (like I am) or loved to play tennis with a passion or had hopes of going to Stanford or dreams, any dreams? Now they will probably never be attained. I mean, here I was in the happiest place on earth and I was reminded that one mistake can screw up your life, or really 3 lives: hers, her boyfriend's (he looked really cute too), and of course the baby's. Just one mistake and everything might disappear. It made me think about a lot of different things. I miss Brad so much.

Kevin

11/14

Te quiero y tengo muchas ganas de verte. (Spanish phrase)
I love you & can't wait to see you again. (English phrase)

Adina is here now and I'd say everything is just right. It was so great to see her after 3 days of being apart. It felt so good just to hold her again and to see her. Yesterday we all (me, Adina, and Jake) went to this kick-ass water park like an hour away & caught some rays & went on all the water park rides. I thought we were having a good time until suddenly I heard someone calling after Jake and when I turned to see who it was I saw my asshole brother Neil. What was HE doing here? Supposedly my mom knew and she told him where to find us b/c she wanted it to be a surprise. The thing is everyone knows that *I CAN'T STAND MY BROTHER.* I felt like it was the shittiest surprise and that my vacation was ruined. I told Adina that too. It isn't like I haven't given him a million chances to do right by me either. I always give him opportunities to be civil, but he just bothers me nonstop.

So all I wanted to do was *LEAVE* there and Adina and I booked away and made it back to Disney where we hooked up w/Katie again and did some more rides. Later on we went over to Katie's hotel and swam around in the rooftop pool and all for a long time. We just chilled together and it was soooo freakin great b/c there I was in this beautiful place with just her and me. I don't know if it is love or what but I do know this is something I have never felt before and I do think I am in love. That night we all went back for some special late night honker thing at Disney and we all ditched Neil. That was the best part of the trip so far, ditching him. Later on when I took Adina back to her hotel, she told me that I made her really happy. I was really touched by that. She is so nice ta ta, I am out—gotta sleep.

Jake

November 14

Swimming here is so awesome. I could stay in the pool all day. And the Jacuzzi is cool too. I wish I was getting a darker tan here but I'm not. There are a few *HOT* girls here but they're all with their parents and I haven't really been talking to any. I guess what makes this trip so cool is the fact that a whole bunch of friends are down here at the same time. But it sucks because Kevin's girlfriend Adina is always here with us, and when she's around that's all Kevin does is obsess about her. They're *ALWAYS* kissing and hugging. I feel so stupid hanging around them but it's not like I can go anywhere else. Other than Kevin and Adina making out everywhere, the vacation is great. I got my mother a ceramic carousel because she loves those—she has a very big collection. And my giving her something will make her very happy which means that ultimately she'll let me do more stuff and let me go out more.

Katie

I worry so much about Jake sometimes. I know so much is going on in his life but he doesn't ever talk about it. How can he be like that? Sometimes I feel so awkward because I don't know whether to ask about his father's condition. I usually don't, but rather try to do things that will make him happier. I thought we should throw him a surprise party and everyone else said they were up to it. Well, once we decided to go ahead with the plans, we had to pick a date and decide where to have it (my house seemed like the best place since it holds the most people). Our first meeting was set up to discuss invitations, food, decorations, etc. Kevin and Baxter were the *ONLY* ones in our close group of friends who showed up. Em, Sherelle, and Marybeth all went to some football game instead. When they found out about Jake's party of course they claimed we never told them. They blew up for not being involved. But overall it was a real good time for Jake (I think he liked it anyway). I'd never felt so good in all my Community Club volunteering as I did being able to give so selflessly to someone who really needed it. I will never forget how happy Jake looked that night and I really think that if nothing else, the memory of his party will remind him that he can survive all the trials and challenges he will face in the next few years. There are still so many other people who love & care for him. How can you not adore him . . . he's so funny and obnoxious. When we were at Space Mountain getting into the cars, Kevin and Jake were screaming, "I have hemorrhoids" and "Please stop the ride—I can't feel my balls!" It was humiliating, but funny.

Basically we spent the whole afternoon doing everything possible to avoid Kevin's brother Neil in every way we knew how. Apparently Neil came to Disney b/c he wanted to surprise his girlfriend, but he didn't really know where she was staying. All he knew was that she was in Anaheim. Kevin thinks that's just *STUPID* and now he wants his brother *GONE*. I can't imagine feeling that way about my brother.

To be honest, I don't know what to think. This evening when they all got back from the water park, we met up at the Jungle Cruise ride in Disney and my purse got knocked into this low part of the boat when the ride stopped. Fortunately, Neil found it right away. He searched using this bouquet of plastic light-up flowers that he had with him. They were like a pink flashlight—it was cool! Of course after some time passed, Kevin found a way to ditch Neil *AGAIN* and move along. We were back to just us for the time being. To be perfectly fair, I think Kevin blew everything a little out of proportion. I don't know why he has to be so dramatic about it.

Baxter

November 14

Well, tonight I was actually planning to go over to Sherelle's, but she never called me. Sometimes she and I hang out when she's not going with Marybeth to see the boys (that's what she calls them). Hopefully she has a good excuse for blowing me off. Luckily I didn't already rent a movie.

WHY DOES THIS ALWAYS HAPPEN TO ME?

Once again for the millionth weekend in a row Megan did NOT return my beep. I think that was the last time I will ever beep her. Which sucks. I am always the one who has the crushes, never the other way around and for some reason it is always me lately who ends up being *crushed*.

I have soooo much homework that I need to do tomorrow. I hope I get it done. I'm beat.

Emma

11/15, 7:30 PM

This weekend I was away at a church retreat. All of us peer ministers at my church have to take freshmen away on a retreat where we help the younger kids get ready to make their confirmation. Most of the freshmen don't want to be there, but they really have no choice. All the peer ministers have been working really really hard, we've been planning for like 6 months for this. Marybeth was there too.

When we first got to the place where we were staying, we had these things called "large group ice-breakers," and we also played "the machine game," where some people act out an object and everyone else has to guess what the machine is. I acted like a blender and everyone thought that was pretty funny. During one of these group activities one of the kids, Joe, I was working with actually told me to shut up! I flipped out on him and told him that if it happened again, I would send him home. And I didn't even go tell the workshop leader b/c I wanted to give this kid one more chance.

But one of my other friends in the group told me that I was crazy to put up with any shit from a freshman! But I still didn't tell on him, and now I am soooo glad since during the weekend Joe got a little better. Saturday during the peer minister meet-ings we were all gabbing about this exercise called the "We" Wall, when you go away with just one other person and roam and talk. I chose Joe as the one I wanted to go with. I really wanted to find out whether or not he could open up. Much to my sur-prise, he did. He told me a lot about himself and it went well. The feeling that I got after our walk was really hard to put into words.

Later on, we had to make T-shirts with our "We"

Wall partners. Joe and I had a great time. From then on, every time Joe would see me, he would punch me lightly or he would say something funny to my face. I guess the story is that he had changed a lot when his parents got divorced. I guess that makes sense. When the retreat was over, he even gave me a big hug and introduced me to his mom. Everyone around us was shocked about the fact that we had gotten so close in such a short amount of time—especially Marybeth who I didn't see until later on b/c she was in a different group. I REALLY hope me and Joe can keep in touch.

xoxoxoxox Emma

p.s. This week Cliff and I hooked up for the first time, at my computer, actually. We were sitting at my desk looking online and I looked at him and it just happened. Then we hooked up again saying good night by the door. He actually said he would miss me when I went away to the retreat. I think he did too. He e-mailed me even though he knew I would be away all weekend. I totally didn't expect it! He said he was just on AOL thinkin about his "buddy" (who is me) and said he was bummed that we wouldn't be watching *Dawson's Creek* together this week. I am so glad the retreat is over. I have to go online RIGHT NOW to talk to Cliff before I go eat. I am starving.

Marybeth

November 15th

I just got back from our church retreat and I had a blast. I never wanted it to end. Is that weird or what? I feel like a whole new person after these retreats—it's like I'm relieved of everything that's been bothering me and I'm brought back in touch with my faith, like who I am and stuff. It's so great to step back from everyday life and do something totally different. I mean, Emma is always there too, but we don't really have to interact that much.

Overall the weekend was a *GIANT* success, I guess. That's what our leader said. I gave the first talk to everyone about taking risks. I was nervous but then it got easier.

"Why It's Important to Take Chances"
by Marybeth Miller

Some chances we take are big, some are small. We take them every day. The impact of any risk you take can be great. Someone can learn and understand something all because of your help. But the point is, every chance is worth taking.

I'm the type of person who doesn't let anything bother me. If you dish something out to me, I will give it right back. I'm basically a big joker. I am who I am and I can't promise that I will ever change for you. I realize that I'm taking a huge chance just by admitting that. Not everyone can say that. Many people conform to ideas about what others want them to be.

Like teenagers are sometimes so afraid to be their own person, afraid of what others might think or say about them. Well, that's not like me at all. What others think of me doesn't bother me. Yeah, it's nice to be liked, but I am willing to take the risk of *not* being liked. Everyone should try this. It is very freeing to accept yourself and express yourself.

Another risk I take is making people laugh all the time. I guess I think that this is like a gift I have been given. For me, the risk is putting myself out there to make other people feel good, no matter what else is going on. Sometimes I wish I was a little more serious at times, or I wish I could give better advice. Sometimes I wish I were a better basketball player than I am, or wish I could run a little faster at track, or throw a little bit farther. I don't have it all, but I do have a special gift that others don't have. I can make people happy. And I think it is worth taking a million

chances in order to use all of my
gifts. I want to be proud of the risks
I take.

Most of the time, after going out on
a limb or taking a chance, I am never
in the same spot I started out in. In
other words, risk always pays off.

I think we should all start taking
chances this weekend. We can start
stepping aside from our normal, everyday life and try something new . . .
maybe even risk using one of our own
special gifts. It could make a difference in our life and in someone else's
life. And you'll feel better about
yourself.

Katie

November 16
@ 10:20 P.M.

Just two days ago I was in California enjoying
myself with my family and friends in the sun and
now I feel like my life is falling apart. I just can't
take this feeling anymore! Juggling everything is
HELL. But I keep on saying I can't let myself fall! I
must get through it somehow!

I have to make myself feel better. Yesterday I
went to sleep at 2 A.M. so today was a kind of daze
for me. Get some sleep! That's the thing to do.

I have not gotten the results yet for the school competition between Carlos and me and it's all I can think about. I really want to get it, but I don't know what will happen. I THINK the interviews have gone well so far, but we'll have to see what happens. Anyway, I must go to sleep now before I pass out. I hope tomorrow is a little happier than today.

Billy

11-16

Football is almost over. Thank God. Blair D. says I don't call enough but I can't be worrying about what she thinks or whether I call her enough during the week. I don't have time for that. My parents asked me today if I think I am applying myself as much as I could be. What am I supposed to say to that? I am working as hard as I can. Don't they know I am doing the best I can? I'm sick of this. I just hope they don't do anything drastic like take away my privileges or the car or something like that. That would be the worst. Oh, and of course in the middle of everything stupid Ms. Gifford gave me a bad grade on this English pop quiz.

Baxter

November 17

This has been the *BEST* week at school so far, even though it's only Tuesday. I found out that I am getting a B+ in chem and in physics. And I am also starting to understand it, which is even better!

But the best part of the whole week is that I have been talking to Megan on a regular basis. She and I have been seeing each other and talking soooo much in school. All we do is yell and flirt. Last night at hall decorating all we were doing was punching each other on the shoulder and stuff. She pinched me once. It was great.

Gotta do my homework now, but I am so happy so it doesn't matter at all.

I ♡ her so much!

Emma

11/17, 8:30 PM

I had to type a history paper tonite and it took me forever. It was much harder than I thought it would be. And I worked really hard on it but I know my stupid teacher will not give me a good grade because that is the way he is about everything. He is a really bad marker. I really hate history anyway so at this point I don't even care what kind of a grade I get. Actually I do care, but I'm not in the mood to show it.

Right now I am watching a tape of that show *7th Heaven* which I never used to watch but now I think it is pretty cute. This show is about drugs. One of the kids on it is doing some kind of drug. I hope kids who watch learn from this. I think it's a pretty serious issue. A lot of kids in JFK do drugs, I know that. Last year at the end of the year I saw these two guys exchange money and a bag of something. I am not sure what it was exactly, but I know it was something that shouldn't have been going on at school. If I wanted a dime bag or whatever it is called I could just go to a kid at school. Sometimes I wish these kids would just get caught or something. School is not a place for that kind of stuff. I know I sound mean and righteous and all, but that is just how I feel. I have opinions sometimes too.

Kevin

11/17

Be prepared to rise up into the rainbow, far away from the pain of life into measureless space of color, light, and music, where the mind can secure itself and dreams fly free!
—dj zip

69

That quote is the best. It makes me feel soooo awesome. That's what it's all about. Unfortunately I am still having a tuff time dealing with all that shit that happened with my brother when we were at Disney. I have an extremely large headache about the whole thing I just can't stand it at all. It will only get bigger too, I know it.

I really don't wanna be in school this week. Homework sucks the big one. I really miss the 80° weather. I had swimming practice today and since I was just swimming so much in Cali I thought practice would be totally easy but *I WAS WRONG!* I was struggling massively just to stay afloat. I give so much credit to swimmers. Everything here feels exactly the same as it did before vacation. It sucks just as much. Dull and boring nothing good or exciting. That could be also because Adina is still away. She's coming home tonight and we might see each other I don't know yet for sure. I miss her already and it's only like a day or 2 since we saw each other. She is so amazing.

ta ta, for now, Kevin

Jake

November 17
Kevin and I were just talking today about how it is so sad to come back home. But I did miss my

family so I am glad in a way to be back. This morning when I was getting dressed for school I started putting on shorts because I was still in a California state of mind but then I realized of course it is much colder. Ha. Ha.

Tonight I had that new promotion job over at the supermarket. We were passing around these frozen pizzas tonight and I ate like 7 of them. I have been thinking maybe I should study business management in college. Then again, who knows.

I'm a little out of it these days.

Like I felt *REALLY* out of it at school today like I was just going through the motions or something. I waited in the hallway twice before different classes just so I could see Claudia walk by. She didn't see me but she looked SO good. Wow. I miss her a lot.

At the end of the day a bunch of us getting rides all met at the front door of the school. Usually we scream out "shotgun!" and run to the car and most of the time I get to the car first but today was different. Today I let this other girl, Kevin's friend Debbie who gets dropped off first, be the one to ride up front. She's pretty hot. I never really noticed her like I did today. Maybe I should ask Kevin if she's a good person to ask out. I think she might be the right kind of girl for me.

My Perfect Partner

Kevin:

AdinA is the most beAutiful
ever And i Am the luckiest guy
cuz she is A big RomAntic like i Am
into cuddling And All thAt shit

Katie:

I like someone who believes in my
same priorities. Brad and I know how to
support each other, even in stressful times.
The perfect partner knows how to listen.

Teresa:

I am a hopeless romantic. I am
a true believer in signs and
symbols of things that are meant
to be. Right now I don't see ANY
major signs.

Billy:

Girls who don't get obsessed or too
emotional.

My Perfect Partner

Marybeth:

   Just make me laugh. That's all I need.

Jake:

   Claudia. I hope I can get her back.

Emma:

   He should be the one person I can tell
anything to and he will always be there
for me and doesn't need to talk to a
whole bunch of other girls. I hate that.

Baxter:

   For once, someone who likes me as much as I like
them.

Teresa

Dear Diary,

For a week or so now I have been worried that it was way too strange to even think about liking Zach because he is friends with Jake. But now I'm changing my mind. Things with me and Zach are so great (except for the fact that he seems to be obsessed w/sex—*LOL!*).

Wow, do I have a terrible past with guys. My longest relationship was when I was in the 7th grade and I went out with this guy for only 7 months. Otherwise, my longest *REAL* relationship was this past spring when I went out with my friend Gina's friend Rusty (well, his name is Robert but Rusty is what everyone calls him). I know I shouldn't be in a long relationship at this age, but the truth is that all my friends are, and I want to have that too. From what I hear it is a special thing to be in love. I just wish I could experience it for once. I am sick of being heartbroken and alone. I'm ready to find someone special and I am sick of waiting! I don't know what will happen with Zach but I hope everything works out for the best. I hope he can take it slow.

This is a poem I really like that I copied out of *Chicken Soup for the Teenage Soul*. It says all the things I can't say.

After a While

After a while you learn the subtle difference
between holding a hand and chaining a soul
And you learn that love doesn't mean leaning
and company doesn't always mean security
And you begin to learn that kisses aren't contracts
and presents aren't promises
And you begin to accept your defeats
with your head up and your eyes ahead
with the grace of a woman, not the grief of a child
And you learn to build all your roads on today
because tomorrow's ground is too uncertain for plans
and futures have a way of falling down in mid-flight.
After a while you learn that even sunshine burns
if you get too much.
So plant your own garden and decorate your own soul
instead of waiting for someone to bring you flowers.
And you learn that you really can endure
that you really are strong
and you really do have worth
And you learn and you learn
with every goodbye you learn...

—Veronica A. Shoffstall
written at age 19

Marybeth

November 18th

Last night into today wasn't too good. I'm not feeling that strong for some reason. What happened is that Rick Wright, the kid I'm seeing sort of, wanted me to tell him all this shit about the guys I've dated in the past. I didn't want to tell him. That's my business, right? Anyway, for whatever reason Rick wanted to know if any guy had ever tried to have sex with me. Well, that really floored me right there. I mean, what kind of a question is that? I didn't want to lie or anything but I also didn't want to get Rick upset. Of course, he didn't understand that and so then he was barely talking to me or looking at me. What a mess. Well, eventually he felt bad and went out and got me Jewel's new CD. I was so happy because I really wanted it. Jewel is my idol. I think she's the greatest. And now Rick and I are ok and that's all 4 now. We saw each other at hall decorating tonite.

Kevin

11/19

Today is mine and Adina's two-month anniversary and it's a really really good day. I am sooo happy about everything. Today is also T-Shirt Day at school and everyone's supposed to wear some crazy color or message. Yesterday was Hat Day and I wore a big-ass Mad Hatter hat that I got in Disney. It was really cool. Tomorrow isn't anything and Monday is Pajamas Day. It's all part of Verve Week at school. We have this every year and the classes battle to see who is the best. Our grade has won 3 years in a row (including this year—I bet). The only thing we sucked at this year was hall decorating. Ooooh my bad, b/c we may have also done badly on some other stuff. I hope we win anyway.

Okay, so the best thing still is Adina and me. *TWO MONTHS!* Right now with Adina I think I am probably the happiest I have been in a long time, prob. ever as far as relationships go. Adina has said stuff to me about the fact that she isn't ready for sex and won't be for a long time but I pretty much feel the same so it's cool. That's not what's going on here anyway. It is so much bigger and better than that. For now, I am just grateful to be getting back the sweetness and romance that I give to her. Like she gave me this great card today. She said that I make her feel special all over and that her mom even says she has this glazed over and giddy look all the time now that she and I are dating. She says she has never been as happy as she is w/me.

We made each other this promise on the Disneyland monorail—we said we were meant to be together—and I *NEVER* wanna break that.

I hope Adina's the one.

Jake

November 19

I was supposed to meet Kevin after classes today. He left me this note by my locker that said he couldn't drive me home because he had some surprise thing happening with Adina. I guess maybe it's their 2-month anniversary or that's what he said. I don't know what is going on with them, but it can be really annoying when your good friend decides to do everything for his girlfriend over you. Well, not everything. He is still the greatest guy and I have known him for so long. I would do anything for Kevin—he is like my brother.

Katie

November 19
@ 2:30 A.M. (it's sooooo late!)

I swear I would do *anything* for Brad! Today was his birthday and he left me the most awesome message on my answering machine. What happened is that after school he went right to the driving place for his license and when he passed he went to a phone and called ME! He left me the most adorable message. He said, "I passed! I love you more than anything and I will pick you up after school." I looked forward to his coming all day!

After he picked me up, we came back to my house and I gave him his presents. I got him a key w/my heart (the same kind of thing that Kevin and Adina gave each other) and put a picture of us inside it. Then I also got him a sweater and tickets to this musical we both wanted to see. He said he liked EVERYTHING. And then being in the car ALONE with him was weird but really, really nice. His car is beautiful. His parents got him a dark blue Jeep. I love how nice it is but of course I wouldn't care if it was a piece of junk.

Then we went out to dinner with his parents. It was the first time I have met them so I was kind of nervous. But I know I made a good impression. When we were out, I almost wanted to tell them that I am in the top of my class *and* head of all these groups at school, but I can't bring myself to tell anyone. I mean, Brad knows all that stuff, but I try to hide it as much as possible because it really changes the way people look at me. I want to be seen as a normal kid—not as a nerd or a genius. At first I was actually reluctant to tell Brad any of that stuff about me, but I decided that if our relationship was going to be long term, I had to. He took it really well and respects what I do and how much I accomplish but I just asked him not to tell his friends about all of it. Once I got teased so badly because Brad came to visit my school with some of his friends (they were coming to watch tennis) and they saw this bulletin board at school that had all these school newspaper clippings showing my name and picture. They teased me so much for that.

Anyway, his family was very nice to me. We went to a fancy restaurant for dinner and Brad even said he would take me back there sometime just the two of us. I slept in his arms the whole way home. When I finally got back home late, I tried to do some homework (I have so much to do for class tomorrow) but I ended up drifting to sleep about 1:30 I think. The reason I am still up writing about all of this is because I woke up a while ago and I can't fall back to sleep.

About twenty minutes ago (at like 2 A.M.) the phone rang and woke me up. It was Brad. He said he couldn't wait until tomorrow to talk. He was sitting in his room reading this card I gave to him and he said he started crying because he felt so moved. Isn't that cute? I am so tired but so happy.

Emma

11/19, 6:25 PM

I think things are going really good with me and Cliff. We're gonna hang out tomorrow nite (Friday) and this time he was the one who asked me out. I was so excited! Too bad he is going away for the rest of the weekend (from Sat. to Tuesday), going with his pal Josh to visit his sister at college. I told Cliff he wasn't allowed to hook up with any college girls and he laughed at me. He always laughs when I say things like that. *HE NEVER TAKES ME SERIOUSLY.* He says that he does, but I don't think he really does. I am really going to miss him a lot over the weekend. He said he would get me a present. I just wish I knew what was going on with the two of us.

I think I'm feeling bad in general too because of everything that's going on still with Marybeth and Sherelle. Today was a really bad day with my friends. At lunch this kid Rick was making fun of me. He always is, it's kinda the way we relate. Anyway, he kept doing it so much that it started to bug me and instead of having Marybeth and Sherelle—my 2 best friends—sticking up for me, they were just laughing too. That really hurt because of all people they should have been the ones defending me. I even heard Marybeth say, "Listen to what he is sayin!" and she was laughing her head off. So was Sherelle.

I was like—here I am being left out AGAIN from their stupid jokes only this time it was worse because it was like *I was the joke.* So later in 6th period I sat right in front of the two of them and said nothing. I just have to ignore them is what I told myself. And then Sherelle walked right up in my face and said, "Are you mad at me because I didn't tell Rick to shut up?" Whatever. I ignored her. And then she got all snotty with me and kept saying I had no right to be mad at her because she had nothing to do with Rick only by this time she was literally *yelling at me*. So I yelled right back. And then of course we went to science lab and we had to pick partners and I got someone else b/c Sherelle and Marybeth were together. We didn't say much for the rest of the school day.

An hour ago I was just on the phone again with Sherelle and we were talking like everything was normal so I guess she's not mad anymore. Why did she get so mad to begin with? And why at me? I didn't do anything wrong. They were *MAKING FUN OF ME*! I tried to call Marybeth but only got her machine and left a message. She better call me back.

This stuff keeps happening and I just don't know how to fight back. And they know I can't. I feel like sometimes I am losing my 2 best friends and that is really scary. I mean I know that your friends are supposed to change in high school, but the three of us said we would ALWAYS stick together. We have been through so much already. It can't be thrown away just like that, can it? I'm not just blowing everything out of proportion, am I?

Marybeth

November 20th
I feel like I have nothing to say these days. I have been feeling kind of quiet inside. Today was

Color Wars in school. My grade came in first place like we have for the last 3 years. I was in the tug-of-war competition and we won our first tug but lost the 2nd. So anyway, after school five of my friends came over and my dad got sort of pissed off at me b/c we were making a lot of noise. He said it sounded like someone was going to fall through the floor. Anyway, I think I'm gonna call Em and see what she's up to this weekend. Maybe we can go to a football game or something.

Billy

11-20

I can't believe how fast time is going by. Football is taking up like most of my time this fall. After weeks of practicing, *winning is SUCH a great feeling* but losing is depressing. I guess I am feeling a little depressed these days only I am not sure why. No one would really guess that I am because I don't show it to anyone in the outside only maybe a little to my mom or maybe Blair D. a little. It's just hard to know you're putting in weeks of practice for something and you don't even know when or how you will get it back. All this practice in life has to mean something, right? It's like my work too. Even the stupid Color Wars at school. Like for some reason I really wanted to win the 3-legged race, and then Baxter and Kevin won. I didn't even know they could run fast. It was stupid.

Sometimes I wish I had it easy like my brother Lee. He was regional champ and all the power and respect you attain from that is so spectacular. When I see his pictures and articles in the local paper I am so happy for him but I want to be like him. I want to go to Michigan like him. I want to be regional champ too.

And even though what I am feeling is competitive, all that makes me feel closer to him at the same time. I feel like a part of him is hooked up with a part of me. On the night he packed his stuff and left for school and I wept for like 20 min. I had never felt that emptiness like a part of me was leaving and *IT WAS DEPRESSING*. Only after he left home did I realize how much I needed him and needed to talk.

What Bums Me Out

Billy:

Never having enough confidence, even though people think I am so full of myself. I also get annoyed when my parents don't listen to me. They don't get it.

Marybeth:

It's hard not to get bummed out when someone acts 1 way in private, and then when they're around other people they're completely different.

Emma:

It bums me out that some friends always have to get drunk to have a good time.

Kevin:

What sucks the most is distrust, like when you tell someone something And they don't believe you or trust you And then you get into A confrontAtion About it

WhatBumsMeOut

Baxter:
When someone I like makes fun of me. And I don't think my friends know how much it bothers me when they do it. But it does. It really does.

Katie:
Stress, stress, and more stress.

Jake:
A lot lately. My breakup with Claudia and my dad's being sick. Those are the biggies.

Teresa:
I get really, really bummed when I feel insecure, whether it's about looks, or my abilities, or not having a guy in my life, or whatever. I know I shouldn't, but I do.

Teresa

Nov 20 (9:00 p.m.)

Dear Diary,

Why did this week seem so much longer than last week? I ran into Billy this afternoon at school and he seemed really down. I think he has a lot on his mind. Hey—who doesn't?! This week we had Color Wars so everyone is acting a little crazy! Gina says we've all lost our minds!

Anyway, I saw Billy by the lockers talking to Jake and Kevin and it made me a little bit sad inside. I was thinking again about how much I love all these guys but I can't find Mr. Right no matter what I do or no matter how hard I try. It just makes me so sad. Yeah, right!

I was listening to the Goo Goo Dolls just now and I think that song "Iris" is so good. "And I don't want the world to see me 'cause I don't think that they'd understand. When everything's made to be broken, I just want you to know who I am." That describes me, all right.

I wrote this poem tonight. I don't know really who the poem is about and I don't mean to be coming off soooooo sad inside b/c I am really feeling pretty good. I mean, I know things will work out for the best and that I have an okay thing going now with Zach. He seems to be a little bit fixated on the whole sex thing, but what guy isn't, right? I guess I am just mistrustful deep down.

WONDERING

I wake up one morning
After such a long night
Looking at my reflection
I wonder if I am all right

If I knew I would lose
The love that I sought
I would not have spoken
I would never have thought

I know something about me
Just isn't quite right
And even when I pray
I still cry every night

I gave my love away
And you never gave it back
You took part of me with you
Will you ever give it back?

I wonder almost always
Why it was that you picked me
You had me thinking about the future
Thinking about what might be

And now your love is wandering
I know you're moving on
I'm wondering how not to be sad
Now that you have up and gone

Baxter

November 20

I have been wondering a lot about Megan. I mean, she still hasn't returned any of my beeps, but now I'm thinking that it's really more of a game. I know there is something between us because we constantly talk and flirt. Today she even asked when my birthday was and asked if when I got my license could I drive her around? I said *OF COURSE*!!!

By the way, today our school had Color Wars and we won for the 3rd year in a row. *YEAH!* And the best part was when Kevin and I won the three-legged race. It was so great! Everyone was cheering Baxter! Baxter! Baxter! And when we won the 2 of us went absolutely crazy! Megan even gave me a hug, which made up for not returning my beeps all week.

Katie

November 20
@ 4:00 P.M.

Let me start by saying that I had the *GREATEST* day ever! I got up at 6 this morning to shower and then I was off to school and first period I got called down to guidance. Guess what!!!? I beat Carlos and got the position for the Intrastate School Committee!!! I am soooo psyched! Don't get me wrong—I know I have a long road ahead of me. I mean, I may have gotten picked at my school and now I have to go through county, area, and state evaluations and then only 100 out of 450 get picked. But what an honor to be nominated. And I knew I was the best candidate.

And that was only first period. Then during second period today I was anchor on the JFK morning show that's broadcast over the TVs in the classes & lunchroom. I wasn't even paying attention at one point and my coanchor actually read off my name! "Congratulations to Katie Carson for being selected the top player for All-Conference Tennis at the coaches meeting last night." I had suspected our team might win something but nothing had been confirmed and then to get my own award was such a surprise. Hooray! I was so excited!

Later on we had Color Wars (last period, actually) and we had to organize and run them. Of course they went really, really well, since the Class of 2000 WON! This girl Leslie and I had to carry the 50-pound tug-of-war rope back. What an adventure! Then I came home and I had a 2-hour tutoring session for math.

Tonight Brad picked me up and we went over to Tim's house. Everyone was drinking and I felt uncomfortable but I was so proud of Brad because he didn't have a single sip. He was driving! We left around 9:30 since there was not much going on. There we were with a means of transportation (finally!) and we didn't know what to do! I just hope I can stay "up" and keep feeling as good as I have felt for the last few days, especially over this weekend.

Jake

My weekend is kicking ass like no other! Friday during school was the Color Wars and this is a game against all of the other grades and we WON and were all psyched. Friday night we all went to the movies to see *I Still Know What You Did Last Summer* and this is who was there: Mick Lazlo, Micky Geffen, Jonny, May, Debbie, Diana Russo, and of course Kevin and Adina. The movie was ok but I was pissed because there is gonna be another sequel and I want to know what happens to Jennifer Love Hewitt since I love her.

After that we went back to May's house and hung out. We got hungry so we went to the A&P and bought this huge Entenmann's coffee cake and ate it in like a minute. By that time it was time to come home so I got in about 12:00 AM as usual. My parents don't care usually if I come in a little late because I have been a good boy lately.

All day today was pretty boring though. I didn't

do much except talk to this girl Diana Russo that I might hook up with. I did go over to Lazlo's to shoot some pool and watch *Armageddon*. That turned out to be pretty cool because I actually won $3.00 in pool and the movie really kicked ass. Kevin's girlfriend Adina was crying and that made me laugh, and then Lazlo was jokin around so I laughed even harder. He was saying stupid stuff and acting out the movie and it was funny. It was great to be around my bunch of best friends. Of course, like I said Kevin's girl Adina was there too but that's ok I guess. It was still fun even with her hanging on his arm all night.

Kevin

11/21

Yesterday a whole bunch of us went to see *I Still Know What You Did Last Summer* and that was a really awesome movie except the ending blew because they *STILL* are keeping you in suspense, so I know I am just gonna have to see the next one. Then all day Sat. *we just chilled* and at night went over to Lazlo's house b/c Friday was his b-day and he wanted some help, like having friends around with your family is the best. All the guys me, Jake, Lazlo, Micky Geffen, and Jonny were hanging and that was fun. Of course also there were Adina (looking really hot!), Lazlo's woman Deb, and this girl Diana Russo who I think was a chick that Jonny wanted to hook up with. Today I just woke up and did the usual which was hung out w/Jake and chilled. I also had to clean up the basement b/c my dad asked me to.

Marybeth

November 21st

This morning first thing my mom drove over to Ticketmaster to get me a ticket to this cool Starlight Christmas Concert but they were already sold out. I was bummed. Later on this morning at 11 I fed the homeless and then I babysat until 4 and now it's about 7:40 and I am waiting to go out. I'm going to a party tonight at my friend Liza's. My mom told me she didn't want me drinking tonight so I don't think I will, even though it's supposed to be a drinking party.

Last night I went to the mall, ran into some friends, and we headed over to 7-Eleven to hang out for a couple of hours. *My life is fun, huh?* Sometimes it is, sometimes it isn't (ha ha). Anyway, I'm waiting for my ride—and I just hope Liza's party doesn't get busted.

Emma

Last night I had so much fun and all I was doing was hanging out with my cousin Barb and her friend Karen who drinks a lot. I don't know what Marybeth or Sherelle were doing but whatever. Anyway, we all wanted to drink, so we went into Karen's room at her house so her mom would have no idea what we were doing. We were drinking something mixed with Snapple and it tasted so good. We all got *so wasted*. Of course Barb agreed to be the designated driver and she drove us around even though we didn't really have anywhere to go. We stopped off at 7-Eleven and everyone was there, and since I was in such a good mood I think everyone knew I had been drinking. Of course no one cared because they all were drinking too.

Oh, and I made Barb stop the car at Cliff's house too because I just wanted to see him one more time before he left for the weekend. He knew I was drinking too, and he laughed at me like he always does. Before we left though he gave me this big goodbye kiss and I felt so happy because I didn't expect him to do that. Later on when I got home, at like 11:30, I went online one last time to say another goodbye, and he got on the computer too so we were actually talking online. Then we got off and talked on the phone until like 2:15 or so. I think he was drinking with his buddies too and we kept saying how we were going to miss each other so much. It was so awesome. He promised that no way would he hook up with any other girls while he was away. Of course that made me so psyched because I would die if he did that.

Anyway, we eventually both got so tired we were falling asleep practically on the phone and then he said he had to go and so did I and then I said "good night" and then he told me that he loved me. I was so surprised by that and of course I said I loved him back and we decided that we would hang out next week on Wednesday since we have a half day of school before Thanksgiving.

Things are going so well and I just don't want to jinx anything if I can help it. I mean if he didn't have any feelings for me he wouldn't be calling me so late and talking until like 2 in the morning and asking me out, would he? He is just really nice and sweet and I want to go out with him so much. I haven't found a guy that I really like in a long time. I don't want to mess this up.

Marybeth

November 22nd
Okay, Liza's ended up being fun but the truth is I got *SO PISSED* at Rick Wright! He made me so

mad. I had talked to him and mentioned that I was heading over to Liza's but he wasn't going b/c Liza did NOT invite him b/c they don't get along. But then Wright got all pissy with me about the whole situation. He was saying that I was going and I didn't want to see him. And I guess that was a little true b/c I am always hanging with him. Well, he showed up at Liza's looking 4 me which was no good, of course, because by then I was back at this other friend's place. Then Wright went *there,* and by then I had turned around and gone back to Liza's. He went all around everywhere looking 4 me over and over and I hate that. Eventually we ran into each other. I was so mad b/c I wanted to hang out with my friends just for one night and he was supposed to go off and deal with his friends. Instead he has to chase after me. That pisses me off.

Emma

11/22, 6:30 PM
I made 35 bucks last night babysitting and the thing is that I was only there for like 4 hours so I should have gotten only 20 dollars. Whatever. I needed the money. *SO* today I bought a pair of black shoes. I was so sick of borrowing Sherelle's all the time. I'm going to a Sweet 16 next Saturday, so I

also got this cute blue top from the Gap but of course now I found out that Katie is wearing the same exact one so I guess I better find something else fast.

Marybeth just called me and she was complaining about Rick Wright, but I don't understand her. She says she doesn't want a boyfriend but then she totally led this guy on for a whole month. Now she says she doesn't know what to do or tell him b/c suddenly she doesn't really like him. Last night I guess she went to hang out with some friends and he followed her and found her. I think Wright is a little crazy b/c he doesn't understand that she might just want to be friends. Like he is stupid and will not get the hint and I feel bad for her. I knew he would do this if they got involved. I saw this coming. When we got off the phone just now, Marybeth said she was gonna go call him and set things straight again. I'm supposed to call her back in like 15 to 20 minutes to see how everything worked out. I really hope he understands and that she doesn't get too upset. He puts her through a lot sometimes and he can be hurtful.

She says I am the only person she can talk to about this and that Sherelle just doesn't understand the whole situation. That's b/c Sherelle always pushes the issue of Marybeth having a man, especially Wright. Sherelle just wants someone to hang with her and Bobby, that is all she cares about. She's only worried about having someone around to fill her social calendar. She'll just keep on telling Marybeth to try it out and not to worry.

The truth is that Marybeth better bail on Rick Wright fast b/c a lot of other guys are afraid to even go near her for fear of getting beat up. They think Wright will go crazy on them if they try anything with "his" girl. If only Marybeth could just tell Rick and everyone else what she is feeling deep inside. So much could change.

Teresa

Nov 23 (8:40 p.m.)

Dear Diary,

I know most people in our class think college is all about partying and fun but I know it's not. This past weekend I went with Sherelle over to her sister's college and I was reading an assignment that one of the girls up there was trying to finish. I have never seen so much hard work in my whole life. And this was at a state school! I am thinking I want to go to an Ivy League school and I can't even understand someone's freshman assignment at a state school?

I realized this weekend how scared I am to go away to college at all. My hopes were to go to the University of North Carolina, but I don't know what's happening now. I think it's better to stay closer to home, right? I mean, if I need last minute items or money, how am I supposed to get it? I can't make my parents come out every time I need something. I have to rethink my whole idea about going to college.

I am basically terrified about the whole situation. I don't know if I can cut going away and dealing with the pressure there. Maybe I should just stick closer to home and play it safe. Oh, well. Just another pain about growing up. I'd better get used to it. School isn't always gonna be so easy as it is right now.

Baxter

November 23

Today I literally failed my physics test. I don't know what the hell is going on. *I feel soooo lost* in school right now. No matter how hard I study I just don't get it. Nothing is going right right now. I wish I knew why.

Katie

November 23
@ 7:00 P.M.

LIFE IS STILL GOOD! I got my grades today. I wasn't supposed to, but the principal pulled them up for me which is fantastic. I got a B+ in AP chemistry, a B+ in math, an A in AP English, and an A+ in *everything* else. I was psyched! If I keep this up, my rank will be #2 by the end of the year. And I already know that I am carrying a heavier course load than the people who are currently #2, #3, and #4. The best part of everything is that I am not killing myself over good grades. I think I am just blessed with natural brightness! Well, I definitely think that I am the happiest I have been in a long time. When I think back to how I felt last year at this time I have come SO far.

- I am having an awesome marking period.
- Made Conference Champions in tennis
- Tennis team is 3rd in All-Area Competition
- Nominated for the most prestigious of the Intrastate School Committees (which means I will be ranked one of the best students in the state!)
- Managing a full load of extracurriculars

When I went to my college counselor this week I was feeling kind of worried and she said, "Katie, you don't have to worry about picking a college, you can go ahead and pick a dormitory . . . in fact, we'll indicate which one you want on your application." I want to go to Stanford so much, it's like everything I want in one place. My counselor wants me to get into Harvard so I can reject them. I just keep thinking about this quote that I heard a long time ago:

IF YOU'VE BUILT CASTLES IN THE SAND
YOUR EFFORT NEED NOT BE WASTED.
NOW PUT YOUR FOUNDATIONS ON THEM.

For the past 16 years I have been trying in every way I know to reach those castles and Stanford would be it for me. It's a long shot, but I have to try!

Billy

11-23

I am so pissed. I found out that I am going to be getting a B+ in gym. I don't understand that because I've had an A+ in gym my whole time at school. I have to talk to my gym teacher about this. My other grades are okay I guess, but I still can't get past the gym thing. This year football really kind of sucked too. It seems that we're Lodge's (the football coach) worst team that he has ever coached. We have a 3–6 record so far with our final game left to play. Isn't that crazy? What a distinction. Hey, after Wednesday's game, at least I won't have to worry about football 7 days a week. Maybe then I can bring some of my other grades up and concentrate on academics rather than football.

Oh yeah—I started driving on my own on Mon. *FINALLY!* I already hooked up with Blair D. in my car. Things are looking up in that department.

Baxter

Baxter

November 24

Billy was kind of a jerk to me in school today. He was talking about his grades for some reason and I happened to mention that I got an A in gym. He lost it on me! He was so mad because he only got a B+. I was secretly psyched. He always makes fun of me for everything including not being athletic, but now I have the better grade.

While he was going off on me, he said some not so nice things about the way I looked, which bothered me. I am so self-conscious and he knows that. Ever since freshman year I have felt this way. Back then, I was teased for not wearing the right "brand" of clothes and since then I make sure I look good no matter what else. I care too much about what other people think. I want to have some kind of style.

Edward Baxter + Megan Randall

Bax & Megan

E.B.
+
M.R.

Baxter loves Britney Spears!

H o w D o I L o o k ?

Billy:

My friends say I wear khakis too much but they look good and I can't live w/out them. The girls love it at least.

Baxter:

I always wear my Old Navy sweater because it is so comfortable and it just makes me feel good. Megan told me once that she liked the way I dress.

Emma:

Hair is really important and my nails too. They have to be perfect! As long as people tell me I look good, I feel good.

Kevin:

i wEAR stuff thAt looks cool when you're dAncing like this club shirt I love with this All over weird design, plus All my Rings And my 2 fAve necklAces, silver of course

H o w D o I L o o k ?

Katie:
I'm usually pretty conservative. I like to be pulled together because it's so important to make a good first impression.

Marybeth:
My comfy Polo shirts 4-ever no doubt about it.

Jake:
I love suits, club clothes, and bulky shoes.

Teresa:
Personally, I love having a good hair day like when it bounces. I'm a Contempo Casuals kind of girl. I even got voted best dressed in 8th grade!

Katie

Well, I am still as happy as can be. No one can take this away from me! Apart from being so happy about my grades and school, I am on the biggest high because I have the most *WONDERFUL* boyfriend. Brad is *always* here for me no matter what. I am just starting to trust him with everything. Up until this point there is only one person I feel I can tell everything about myself to and that's my friend Jaclyn Roome who's at college. I can tell her—well, and my mom—almost everything. But now there's Brad. I am still a little bit afraid of getting hurt by him. I am not one to wear my heart on my sleeve, but rather I tend to lock it up and rely upon my brain.

I am just *so scared* of having my heart crushed all over again. In my relationship with Robert *I NEVER* felt like this at any point. I'll never forget how good this feels.

I don't know if what I have with Brad is love or what, but it's like my heart is bursting whenever I see him. But I am too young to have found love, right? No! There's that brain interference again. Which lead should I follow—brain or heart? Brad accepts me for me, and he doesn't make fun of me like some other person I used to go out with.

Sometimes I lie in bed and he doesn't seem real,

but then I turn on my light and see his picture next to my bed and I know that he is real and he's right here next to me. Jaclyn says I should live in the moment and not analyze my feelings so much as I should just accept them. She always seems to know what's right, of course she's 18 and she's already been through all this stuff.

Kevin

BORING!! I feel like I have already done all of this before. *Boring* is all I can say. *What am I doing here?* It's Tuesday, and it just gets more and more boring every day. I don't know why either.

Yesterday me and Jake signed up for lifeguarding class because we all know we'd better get jobs. Down by the beach in the summer is good work. You get to spend all your time in the sun and on wave runners when you have time off and THAT is just awesome. I can just see me and Adina down at the shore—yes! You go to work at like 8 or 10 I don't know which and then you get off at like 5 o'clock and then there's 7 bucks an hour plus one day off a week which seems pretty decent. Of course, I had swimming practice earlier today and it was really really freakin hard. I was hurting a lot after and I can't move so I'm like going to bed. I just wanna sleep and do no work. Night! ta ta, Kevin

Jake

November 24

Hey! Hey! Hey! Yesterday was *so boring*! All I did was rake leaves. *I MISS SUMMER.* Me and Kevin signed up for this lifeguarding course though. I always wanted to be a lifeguard, I guess because it means I get to spend a lot of time by the water and I love the water.

So what else is going on? Not much! Actually one cool thing happened today though which was Student Teacher Day which means one of the students teaches while the teacher turns into the student. Anyway, I got to teach auto shop which is like my favorite class besides chemistry. I took attendance and assigned work for the students. I ordered them around and talked just like our shop teacher Mr. Duffy. Plus I got to miss my other classes. I missed my algebra 2 test and she was mad but I don't care because it was awesome and worth it. I am so glad we have off Thursday and Friday for Thanksgiving.

Teresa

Nov 25 (2:35 p.m.)

Dear Diary,

Yeah, we're *almost* out of school for the weekend! It's the day before Thanksgiving and school *thankfully* is OVER. Actually tonight is the home-coming dance and I don't really feel like going but Gina and Wendy want to so I guess we will. I feel sooooooo fat for some reason! I have nothing to wear either. And of course I don't know what's going on with Zach right now, he's being a little distant. He says that things are moving too slow. Well, we're supposed to get together tomorrow after Thanksgiving. I'm staying here with my mom instead of going with my dad to see his family in Virginia. Because my parents are divorced, I get to choose where I want to go each year. This year, I wanted to hang out near home so I could see everyone when they come home from college.

Sometimes I just feel torn about which to do, be with Mom or Dad. I want both! Anyway, it's pretty funny that I feel that way b/c this morning Mom ripped out my horoscope from the paper. This is so me! (She knows me sooooo well!)

11/25 LIBRA . . . You always see everything from at least two perspectives. It's never easy to balance those scales, especially this time of year! Making decisions can be agony, and sometimes you compromise too much to keep everyone else happy. Around the holidays, just make sure you don't lose that Venus charm and that boy-crazy Libra style!

November 25
@ 2:50 P.M.

Eeeeeeuw! I am in 6th period math class and I just saw Robert in the hallway. What is HE doing back here? I guess he's off from college visiting for the Thanksgiving holidays. Wow, he looks like *CRAP!* He looks *so gross*. His face is covered in dark hair and his head is almost shaved and he just looks so bad. I am so mortified that I ever was with him!

I hate seeing him here again. It makes everything come back. Unfortunately he'll be at homecoming tonight too. It makes it even harder to let go of those bad memories. I hate everything he put me through.

I think I hate him most of all for becoming more and more jealous of me and all my successes at JFK. Everything really started to get worse for us when I tried to audition for the musicals at school. He used to yell at me, "Are you crazy? *YOU* can't act or sing. Why would you want to embarrass yourself like that?" He got angry all the time, for no reason. Plus he said he was the only one who could do certain activities, not me. He used to say, "Why are you trying to take something away from me?" He demanded I drop out of chorus, plays, and even Community Club at one point. At one random audition for the school musical (which I decided to try for even though Robert had warned me not to), he started yelling at me right there in front of my music teacher. It was awful—and weird, and that was only the beginning.

A month into rehearsals, we were really close to breaking up. I remember this sooo clearly like it was just a few days ago. It was after the holidays and we both had gotten to school at like 7 A.M.—really early because of all the stuff we always had to do. I remember we were walking up the stairs in the direction of his locker and I said something that made him upset. He grabbed me and pushed me up against this landing in the stairwell where no one else was around. He even restrained my arms so I couldn't move. And he had this cruel, evil look in his eyes. He was screaming at me louder and louder and it was echoing in the stairs, but he wouldn't stop and I was getting more and more scared. Then all of a sudden his arm drew back and he slapped me. It hurt so badly, I can't even describe it. It was like all the bad moments we had ever had came together in that one moment. I could see then this had to end. It was over. Then someone opened the door on the landing above us and started coming down the stairs. Robert just bolted off.

I was sitting there alone, not knowing where to go or who to talk to. The first person I saw on my way back to the main locker area was Kevin. I told him what had happened and he said, "Should I kill him now or wait until later?"

Right then it was so hard to even breathe. But I was proud of myself in a way because I felt like I had friends who cared about me, and I had the

110

strength to walk away from this guy, to walk away from a bad relationship, finally.

Marybeth

November 25th (late)

Rick Wright has been driving me crazy lately. Tonight was the worst.

Me, Sherelle, Bobby, and this guy Eddie were supposed to connect after the bonfire and homecoming dance. Eddie is Bobby's cousin who's here from Texas. So anyway, at the bonfire Rick Wright was like what are *YOU* doing here? So then we went over to the homecoming dance and *HE KEPT FOL-LOWING US!* Wright was asking me where I was going next and I kept saying I am going home (so he would go away). I told him to just relax. Then he asked me if *he* could take me home and I was like *WHAT???!!* I said no, I was going home with Sherelle and we were stopping at her house first to get something. Then he started yelling at me and I got so pissed off. I felt really bad too b/c after yelling at me he started yelling at Bobby and Eddie. It was a big mess. I don't know what Rick's problem is.

Of course what happened after that made up for everything. Eventually Rick bailed and the four of us actually went back to Bobby's house and watched *Dawson's Creek* for a while. It was pretty lame though and we stopped watching. That's when Sherelle and Bobby decided to go upstairs to Bobby's room. They left me there with Eddie. Not to worry though b/c me and Eddie used the time *very wisely*. He is so *HOT*! Of course, he's leaving to go back home on Sat. I can't believe it b/c we really clicked in the same way that Sherelle and Bobby get along so well. Eddie is as big a wiseass as me. Oh well, I'm gonna try to get some sleep before Thanksgiving. I'm going to a football game tomorrow and it's supposed to rain.

Billy

11-26

We lost another football game. Shit. Our record *REALLY* sucks now. Man, if I were Coach Lodge I would kick all of our asses or quit his job or something. I can't believe we did so badly. Plus it was raining which only made it that much worse. Hey, at least it's over. The only really sucky part was that my brother Lee came to the game. When *he* was on the team I don't think they *EVER* had a losing record.

Today my family came over for some great Thanksgiving cooking which was good. Then around 8:00, my bro and I went to see this action movie, *Enemy of the State*. It brought up some questions in my head like things that make you think about life around us, life today.

I guess if I had to summarize the past few weeks, my life is pretty great (apart from football that is). But I am sure something will mess up my mood, since we have a term paper due soon and there will only be more and more work as time goes on. Oh well, that's just how it is. Later.

marybeth

November 26th

I really messed up. I think I may have ruined some friendships. Last night when I hooked ↑ with Eddie at Bobby's house, I didn't really think so much about what I was doing. I mean, I didn't think it mattered. Anyway, this morning I went on AOL and saw an e-mail there from Rick Wright about how he doesn't understand what's going on with him and me and that he likes me so much. After he saw me at homecoming and I was blowing him off, he wanted to know what am I thinking? So I wrote back, and told him the truth. I told him I was sick of him being obsessed. I said a bunch of stuff I wish I could take back. I told him how much it pissed me off when he followed me to this party 2 weeks ago and other stuff. I also told him that I *did* go out after homecoming. I didn't go home at all. I just needed some space.

As soon as I got offline he called me up and he

was crying. He kept asking and asking me who was I with and I didn't want to tell him. But then stupid me told him about Eddie. And when Wright asked if Eddie and I hooked ↑, I said yes, which was a *SUPER STUPID MOVE*.

Immediately he assumed that it was all a setup by Bobby. He blamed Bobby for the whole thing. What Wright said actually was that he knew I wasn't a bitch like all the other girls at school, but that if I valued him as a friend I should have told him what was on my mind. And then he said he didn't think there was any way that we could be friends anymore after this. That really hurt. I mean, it's not fair to say we can't be friends anymore when I was only being honest. I told him everything and I thought that was what he wanted and he's just using it against me now.

Tonight after Thanksgiving dinner, I went over to 7-Eleven to grab something and I saw some of Wright's friends there and they were total jerks to me. They cursed me off and were like, "Oh, where's Eddie?" and then they said that maybe if he were around they'd beat the shit out of him.

And that's not the worst part, because now they're also pissed at Bobby and they say he's a backstabber to Wright. I feel like I really let Bobby down. He says I shouldn't worry about it, he forgives me, but the reality is that I really fucked up.

And then I get this e-mail from Wright that claims I'm too stubborn to ever listen to him and I don't care and most of all I really don't deserve him. Wright says he's been sweet and nice and look what I still did—and I shouldn't even bother saying how sorry I am, because if I really meant it I would do something about it.

God! I don't know what to do. I have never had this problem. It's not like me to let people down. I like making people feel better not worse. Maybe I should have been more careful not to let him think we could be together like bf & gf.

This may go down as the worst Thanksgiving ever.

Emma

11/26, 7:00 PM

Well, my Thanksgiving was really cool and nice. At 2:00 we went to my cousin's house on my dad's side. The only bad part was that Mom had to stay home because my little brother Ronnie has the mumps.

I have so much fun at my cousin's house. They live down by the beach and we only see them this one time a year. I was so hungry when we got there I ate like *EVERYTHING* on the Thanksgiving table. I never eat that much except today.

Afterwards we went back home and Dad stayed with my brother while Mom came with us to go to her sister's place. And then we had to eat all over again! There were so many people there. We all sat at these different tables. I was so full but I ate some mashed potatoes and chocolate pudding pie. I love being with so much family. It feels really good and safe.

Teresa

Nov 26 (11:26 p.m.)

Dear Diary,

HAPPY JURKEY DAY!

Today I went with my mom to her friend's house for Thanksgiving. Last year my mom was there too, but I actually went with my dad to visit his brother and family in Virginia. This year I ate sooooo much! I knew I would! I only stayed at my mom's friend's house until like 6, because I went over to Sherelle's house like I do every year.

Now this is pretty strange b/c Sherelle used to be good friends with our other friend Betsy, only now they don't talk. This is *EXTREMELY* weird because Betsy is Micky Geffen's sister, and Micky is one of Kevin's very best best friends.

Anyway, we all used to get together on Thanksgiving, which was *AWESOME*, but now

Sherelle is stuck with a smaller group because Micky & Betsy decided to have their own group over at their house. It's weird. Like Kevin, Jake, Baxter, etc. all went over to Micky & Betsy's place instead of Sherelle's and that put me in an uncomfortable position. I mean, Marybeth was there at Sherelle's of course, but mostly we were hanging out with this new group of girlfriends Sherelle has—who are not my regular pals. Actually they are known as the sluts of our grade, aka "The Mix." It was different, that's for sure.

Right now I am still full and stuffed with desserts and all kinds of food. I do kind of regret not going to Virginia w/my dad like I always do. I miss my family there, especially since I don't see them that much to begin with. I don't think I will get another chance to go there until the spring either. The reason I am glad I stayed home is to see my friends from college, although I don't know what we're really gonna do this weekend.

As far as Zach goes, things are okay except for the fact that he's *still* dropping all these comments about sex. I mean, he's not pressuring me (I don't think), but he did say that he really WOULDN'T WAIT MORE THAN A MONTH for it. Actually, that kinda scares me. I know my other guy friends like Kevin wouldn't be like that. I don't know.

Kevin

I am so wiped out and my whole family has like
invaded our house. Thank God my 'rents let me
sleep in until like 1 in the afternoon or else I would
die. I can't handle the whole family crowd dynamic.
Like my aunt. She is just so annoying, she just
walked in my room right now. She is one of those
kinds of people who order you around in your own
house. I really hate that. But to be fair, she's actually
pretty cool most of the time. She has 2 adopted
kids, one of which is my godchild.

Wow. My family on Thanksgiving is like this
TOTAL MIX-UP—it's pretty hard for all of us to
keep everyone straight sometimes. There's me;
Larry (my dad); Brita who is my mom; my stepsis-
ters Joelle & Melissa; my stepbrother Roger (who is
this awesome artist I talk to a lot b/c he inspires
me); my dad's sister and her hubby and two kids;
my *REAL* sister Helene and brother Neil (who I
HATE); and last but not least my other adopted sister Zoe who came from Korea.

Zoe is like this miracle baby. She was really sick
and my dad & mom adopted her. Usually she is
pretty quiet but sometimes she can be a nuisance.
Still I love her. I love all of them, except Neil.

And yeah, someone else I am thinking about a
lot today is my other adopted sister Lena. It's hard

to think about her for too long because she was killed. It's such a long story and it's pretty scary to talk about. A fucking drunk driver hit her is all. I miss her. She would be 24 if she had lived. She died when she was only 16, my age, which is *SO FREAKIN UNFAIR.*

So there we all were today (except Lena) for the Thanksgiving dinner, and we all sat squashed together and made small talk and ate food. Busy busy busy.

A bunch of us watched a movie and then afterwards I bailed and went to Adina's house. Later on I met up with friends over at Mick Geffen's, and Jake and me and the rest of the crew all chilled out there until now.

I guess it's been a pretty cool Thanksgiving.

Jake

November 27
Just got back from Micky Geffen's place for dessert with Kevin and Baxter and some of the other guys. Betsy invited over some of the girls too, but Teresa and Marybeth blew it off. It was fun though since a lot of us were there. Even my old friend Chris Smith was back from college and made a surprise visit.

I can't believe it rained today on Thanksgiving. I

119

was planning the whole week for my uncle Charlie to bring his '78 Porsche so I could drive it but he didn't bring it because of the stupid rain. So I didn't get to drive but I still had an okay day.

This afternoon was the only rough part because we ate dinner in the upstairs dining room, and so my brother and I had to carry my dad in his wheelchair upstairs. Yeah, that was probably the worst part. I still just wish my dad could walk and do all the stuff he used to do. Mom's cooking was really good. My family and my aunt's family were there and we sat and had a good time. Of course I was the jokester like always trying to make everyone laugh and have a good time. We watched football later and played checkers. I'm ready to crash.

November 27

Well, yesterday was Thanksgiving and my family came over. We squeezed 12 people into our tiny living room. It was pretty funny. My brother actually had to go out the deck door in order to walk around the house to go to the bathroom.

Last night I went over to Mick Geffen's house for dessert. I guess I had fun but I felt a little left out. Jonny, Kevin, Jake, and Mick tell each other everything and they never tell me. They actually asked me to leave at one point so they could all talk. But it's all water under the bridge. Actually, today I went with Kevin, Jake, and Billy to KFC for lunch. Billy was being kind of a dick and teasing me as usual, but I just ignored it and played along. I don't think he knows how much that bothers me. Well, it's not like I'm gonna make a big deal out of it though.

I still think it is so weird driving with my friends and having just us in the car. I can't believe we all are getting our licenses! Jake has to wait the longest of all the guys in our group. I think he has almost another year left. I get mine in February on my birthday. After eating we came back to my house and played Bond and the Legend of Zelda on Nintendo 64.

Kevin

11/28

This weekend is turning out pretty cool. Yesterday I had swimming practice in the morning and after that was over I went home and hung out for a while until Billy and Jake came over and then we went to Baxter's house and just chilled and played Nintendo 64 with him. Afterwards we went over to Barnes & Noble and I think that is a pretty fun place to hang out, I was surprised how I thought that. Finally I went home and got ready to see Adina. I rented a movie, *City of Angels,* b/c I had never seen it before and it was a great night. We watched the beginning that I remember but then we started doing some other stuff and got distracted. She looked really good that night and felt good too. Oh, but we did catch the ending though. Today I slept in pretty late again. I didn't wake up until after 2. I know, I know, I feel like a waste of life when all I do is sleep but I could seriously sleep 36 hours straight at any given moment I swear. I need my *SLEEEEEEEP*!

Tonite there was a Sweet 16 at this girl Rosie's house. Rosie is a sweet girl who I hang w/sometimes at school. Anyway, Adina came with me and it was a pretty good party but the DJ wasn't too good actually. It ended at like 11, so me and Adina just chilled and talked for an hour or so and then I spent a little time with Lazlo and Jake. Nothing spectacular to brag about.

Jake

November 28

I think that lately Kevin has been kind of an asshole and ditching the rest of us. He is always being sarcastic and it pisses me, Lazlo, and Jonny off. It's not like he is really part of the best friends crew anymore because everywhere we go him and his *ANNOYING GIRLFRIEND* are there and he does not talk to us. Me, Jonny, Mick Lazlo, and Micky Geffen are there talking and he's off somewhere staying with his girl kissing and hugging and if by some chance he gets up, there is Adina following right behind him. So then of course we all have to stop talking. This past Friday Kevin wanted to borrow these pink plastic dice I bought. They're a joke but they're sort of sexual like in a goofing around way because on one there are the words *blow, kiss, lick, touch, tease,* and *massage,* and on the other one there are the words that tell you where to do it like *body, boobs, nipples, toes, lips,* and then one has a ? mark on it. Anyway, Kevin wanted to take the dice and he was really arguing with me that he needed them a lot but they were mine so I hung on to them. I needed them too and anyway his girlfriend wouldn't be interested in them. But he kept asking and he was really pissing me off. Both Jonny and Mick agree that Kevin has been different ever since Adina and he doesn't ever hang out with us alone.

Anyway, Friday we all ended up chilling out without Kevin and Adina of course. I went over to Lazlo's with some other girls in our grade and I broke out those dice (I never did give them to Kevin, no way). I started rolling and it was basically just me and 2 friends Debbie and Betsy playing. I told Betsy to stop playing because she had a boyfriend and we were all laughing. Then I rolled *massage boobs* and I started massaging Debbie's boobs. She was laughing. Lazlo said he was gonna kill me, but he was kidding. Deb's his girl.

Today was Saturday and it was pretty boring so we just drove around. I spent some more time with my friend Chris who is back from college. We actually drove down this one road at like 110 miles an hour. Then he went over to spend some time with Marybeth. They were pretty close last year too. Later on I was standing outside, not really doing anything when my neighbor's car CAUGHT ON FIRE because leaves got stuck under the car! That was weird and funny too because out of nowhere flames started coming from under the car. Nothing much happened. He put out the fire.

Marybeth

November 28th

I can't stop thinking about Rick Wright. I feel bad.

This is pretty stupid, but I was just playing around and I wrote this.

REGRET

I regret telling you, but lying just wasn't right to do.
Neither hooking up nor hurting you was planned,
And just like that the friendship between us was canned.
I don't know how to make this right,
And I do wish I could change the other night.
What I broke is trust, gaining it back is a must.

What I am feeling right now is sorrow,
And I wish that things would get better tomorrow.
Not realizing all the wrong things I've done,
Trying to think of ideas to fix them, but finding none.
I regret what I've done,
Though it really turned out to be one night worth the fun.
I wish I could make this right
But for now I will just stay out of everyone's sight.
It was my wrong choice,
And now I can't even hear your voice.
I don't know what you want to do
Or if you want me too
But how I wish I could talk to you.
Now I wish I could talk to you.

MakeAWish MakeAWish

Marybeth:

I wanna appreciate things that are going on around me more. And sometimes I wish I looked different.

Kevin:

i'm wishin' for world peace of course

Katie:

First, I wish my sister wasn't sick so much. For myself, I wish I could get the #1 ranking in my class. Of course, I make a wish every day to be a better person too. We all should do that.

Teresa:

It would be sooooo great to be a famous author. I got one of my poems published and I hope it is just the beginning! I also wish I wasn't so insecure.

126

MakeAWish MakeAWish

Billy:

  I have to get into a good college like my brother Lee and to win awards and honors and make my parents really proud of me.

Jake:

  I wish my dad was his old self and not sick anymore.

Emma:

  I wish my parents could win the lottery. I also wish I had a convertible and a big house. Oh, and health and happiness for my family.

Baxter:

  I want to meet Britney Spears and get into a good college.

November 29
@ 9:00 P.M.

Thanksgiving weekend almost is over. *WHAT AN EXPERIENCE!* At my house it always is. Every year for turkey dinner (without fail) my grandpa says this really long prayer and by the time he is done dinner is already cold! Every year we go to their house along with all the other members of the Carson family, including the real-life *Brat* Pack, otherwise known as my 7 little blond nieces and nephews. It's usually total chaos and my cousin Sue and I just stayed glued to the sofa watching everyone run around wild around us. The funny part is that there's always a turkey catastrophe and of course once again I have to sit with all the kids and endure mashed potato fights and farting contests. One of these years I'll be seated with the adults, I hope, and learn what goes on there and maybe even have a glass of wine with dinner. Then again . . .

The only bad part of Thanksgiving Day was that Brad overate and fell asleep without calling me. Of course, I was worried and he made me soooo nervous! I hate that feeling but of course I have no one to blame but myself. It's my fault, not his. On Friday he made up for it by taking me out and then going for this long drive together. He parked the car and told me how he felt about me and even played our song. I confessed (finally) to him that I was so afraid of falling for him and getting hurt. That was hard to admit. My feelings are so close to the surface these days.

On Saturday when I went to Rosie's Sweet 16 party, in a way I felt like I was single (is that weird?). I just danced and danced and had a great time. I felt like a complete individual. I didn't know I had it in me to do that. I've been having so many of these mixed feelings lately, like I'm so overjoyed to be with Brad and then moments when I am so glad to have time by myself or time with other friends. Is my mind playing tricks on me?

Like the other night at homecoming, I saw this kid from my neighborhood. His name is Lewis. Apparently he had a crush on me last year and when everything happened with Robert, he and I ended up together. Well, we only kissed once actually, and it was nothing special (he has never had a girlfriend), but there was this *something* between us. So anyway, at homecoming there was Lewis again, and it was the first time I'd seen him in so long— and definitely since I have been dating Brad. Why am I so confused when I know that being with Brad is *the right thing*? I have never been happier, but suddenly I had this feeling about Lewis. I would be so curious to see what could happen between me and Lewis if Brad and I ever separated. Of course that will never happen. I'm just thinking too much again. *I LOVE BRAD!*

Emma

11/29, 1:30 PM

Well, the big news is *ME AND CLIFF ARE OFFI-CIALLY GOING OUT*!! He asked me out this past Friday over the computer, and when he asked me I was shaking. I couldn't believe that this was actually happening. I am so happy. I hope this works out. Friday night when we went out we went over to his house and his mom was so cute because she remembered me from kindergarten! She said I still looked exactly the same. I love his mom. I was so happy to be there in his house with him. And when I left he gave me one of his school pictures and in it he looks so adorable. He also wrote the sweetest thing on the back of his picture about how glad he is to be going out with me.

This has been *SUCH A CRAZY WEEKEND*. I am the ice-hockey manager and we had games *ALL* weekend long. This year I had to manage varsity and JV too and so it's taking up a lot more time. We have to keep up with all the stats from game to game and there are 4 of us managing in all. He also put us in charge of water bottles and we each got our own hockey bag—it is so huge it's like you could fit a person inside it. The only bad part is that it gets so cold at the games I have to remember to wear layers of clothes when I go so I can stay warm.

On Saturday nite I was at this girl Rosie's Sweet

130

16 party (actually Katie and Kevin went too) and it was too long. I really didn't want to go but I was glad I did. We ended up dancing all night. Some kids were a little drunk, but no one really knew that so it really wasn't a big deal. All in all it was a full weekend!

I ♡ Cliff!

Baxter

November 29

I still love Megan, but there is nothing new going on. I haven't beeped her yet over Thanksgiving, but she did promise to call me back.

By the way, for my report card my parents got me a Nintendo game and a gold controller. I love them so much! Here's a list of my grades:

Italian 3 A+
AP English B+
Oceanography A
AP Chemistry B+ BIG SURPRISE!!!
Social Issues A+
Math Analysis A

Honors Physics B+ ANOTHER HUGE SURPRISE!!!
Adv. Photo A
Phys. Ed. A (NO WAY!)
Health A-

Also, this weekend my mom and dad got Chinese food and we haven't had that in a long time and we got these fortunes. Mine said, *"Your ideals are well within your reach."* I usually ignore these but I think my luck is changing, maybe.

Teresa

Nov 29 (5:40 p.m.)

Dear Diary,

Thanksgiving weekend went by too fast. Friday night I hung out with college friends and had a pretty good time, except I noticed that they had all changed a little. Maybe they actually think the same of me. I hate change, but it's a part of life.

On Saturday I was supposed to go out with Zach, but he never called me back and I found out that he ended up hanging out with his ex-girlfriend! I was very, very mad at him and I don't know what more to say, but as of now, things are NOT looking too good. Should I have done more like he wanted to as far as sex? I am so confused.

I did my entire history paper in one night tonight. I am soooo tired of school. I hope this week starts getting better fast.

Marybeth

November 30th

Okay, I talked to Rick Wright again. He finally agreed to talk and the truth is that he *still* wants to hook up w/me. He said he would try to accept me going out with other guys and I told him that I don't think that's right. He is having a very difficult time accepting the fact that from now on we are going to be *JUST FRIENDS*.

There's this other guy I have my eye on right now, actually. His name is Matt. *I REALLY WANT HIM*. Well, I'd prefer Bobby's cousin Eddie (who I hooked up with after homecoming) of course, but he went back to Texas. Anyway, Matt's a senior and he plays ice hockey. I have been talking to him a lot on AOL at night. I always tell him to call me on the phone, but by the time we get to that he's already falling asleep.

Today was my first day of basketball practice. For someone who took last basketball season off, I am pretty good—which made me really happy. But now I am *EXHAUSTED*.

My buddy Chris Smith went back to college yesterday and I miss him already. We got a chance to hang out a little bit this weekend though. And it's okay b/c he'll be home again in like 3 weeks. Sometimes I think about him and me and maybe he is really the one for me. But then again, he's there and I'm here and oh well. Nuff said. I have to go call Baxter, I promised him I would.

Baxter

November 30

Tomorrow my mom puts up the decorations. I love Christmas!

Right now I am listening to Z100. I hope they play Britney Spears. *SHE IS SO HOT.*

School is so much better now that I know my grades were okay. I'm starting to like it again which is the way it's supposed to be, right? I really am starting to understand everything and everything is going fine. Today in lunch I was with Billy and Kevin and some other friends and we talked about *REALLY WEIRD STUFF* like how far would you go to get a million dollars, like what gross and *SEXUAL* stuff would you do? It got pretty disgusting.

As far as Megan goes, I still have no fucking clue what is going on????? She doesn't return my beeps but then she comes up to me all the time to apologize. I just don't get it. I don't get *her.*

Kevin

11/30

I don't get why school got so boring all of a sudden. I don't really like to think about or talk about school so much b/c I dislike it so much. It's like the same shit, different day. Like every day me and Jake hook up and go to school together. Hey, at least now I can drive my phat car and have some freedom, that part of the day kicks (except that the seniors have parking privileges in the school parking lot so I have to get there early and even then I still prob. get a shitty spot).

So today first period was algebra 2 and me and Debbie were mingling before class, but then I spent like the next 48 minutes wondering what the hell I was doing there. So much it's like we *go through the motions* and act like we're doing stuff but really we're not. Anyway then I had gym which sucked too. Ohhh man then I had chem and walked to class with May and Deb. I swear I am sitting in that class every day in like *TOTAL CONFUSION*, like cracking on the teacher (he usually likes and encourages humor), but I'm in the back of the room and he can't really see what I am doing or hear what I am saying. Actually, I can't believe how much every day is like the same thing all over again. I do this *EVERY FUCKING DAY*! And then there's English class and I could go on about that for a million hours like the teacher is soooooo boring, and she's just drooling on about something stupid and doesn't she see that *WE JUST DON'T CARE*!!! Lunch was actually ok today. It was funny b/c we were talking about how much would we need to be paid to do sexual stuff to certain people. It was a sick and hysterical subject, and we were all saying crazy stuff. It was so funny being together like that. I think that lunch is actually the highlight of my day—I know it was today. Of course today history was the last class of the day and I think I fell asleep for part of it. It's usually cool, actually, but for some reason like I was saying over the weekend, I am *SO TIRED* all the time. Next semester might be better since spring is getting closer (sort of) and anyway I will have auto shop instead and that rules according to Jake.

So really I guess I have been doing stuff but really I'm spending most of the time thinking about when I'm gonna see Adina again and what we're gonna do together. I hope I see her after school today but I might just hang out with Jake and Lazlo. Ta ta

p.s. By the way, today in school I wanted to kill Emma she can be such a pain sometimes really. I mean we never get along b/c she is one of these people who acts like someone's friend when they are around but as soon as they leave it's "*BUBYE!*—that's all over," and she's makin fun of them. I hate that, it's *SOO F'ED UP.* If you're gonna say something about someone say it to their face! Mostly I can deal and be mature around her and stuff but today I was in the hall with Marybeth and Sherelle and we were just talking and Emma came over and she was *touchin* me and being all *friendly* and shit and I just wanted her to back off. *I JUST HATE THAT FAKE SHIT.* So Marybeth is pretty cool, and she always defends Emma b/c she says she's a good friend and she's loyal. I dunno I guess maybe Emma's loyal but I don't care. Marybeth says I am just still weirded cuz I hooked up with Em like freshman year or something and I can't deal with having done that. Yeah, well, like time to forget that one thank you very much. Marybeth always knows how to get me for sure. I would hate life if I didn't have her smart ass to count on for sure . . . ok now ta ta, for real

Marybeth

December 1st

Oh my God I want Matt so bad.

He called me tonight but we barely talked. He is such a *HOTTIE* (LOL/laugh out loud!) I can't stand it. Someone called on the other line and so he had to get off the phone and I think he might call back, but I am not getting my hopes up. That makes 0¢.

But I want him.

I have a real big decision to make. I have a ticket to a DMB concert but it's $65 and I think maybe that's a little steep, esp. since I have absolutely NO money. But I wanna go. I don't think I can pull it off. Oh well, I guess I won't be able to make this one. I still looooooove Dave!

Would you not like to be sitting on top of the world with your legs hanging free?—"Lie in Our Graves," DMB (Dave Matthews Band)

Emma

12/1, 3:51 PM

Only 24 days until Christmas! I am so excited. That is my absolute favorite holiday. I am just sitting here waiting for my aunt and the two of us are going to get our nails done. I was just watching my soap opera, *General Hospital,* and it really has gotten stupid. After we go to the nail place, I have to go babysit. I really don't want to, but I feel bad and I can really use the money. Christmas is coming up and I need money to buy gifts for people. The person I babysit for asked if I would help hand out gifts for Santa & Me on Friday. I did it last year and

138

it was pretty stupid. But she said she really needs my help, so my sister and I are both going to do it. It's only until 9 at night, so I will still be able to go out. And luckily it's right near Cliff's house so maybe he will come and get me after. I still have to ask him about that.

Last night I had CCD religion class and it went so well. I realize that I really love to teach and I love my class of kids. Last night me and the other peer ministers had a great class, we were laughing the whole time. The class is so great and the kids are always willing to share stuff with the group. I think it's because they feel safe and know we won't say anything critical or bad. Some of the things are really personal and I don't know if I would be able to share what they share. But I am starting to tell some personal stuff about myself too, so they know me better also. I hope I get this group next year too. I am really feeling lucky these days.

I ♡ Cliff!

Baxter

December 1
Please somebody help me! Luckily I called Emma. I have known her for so long and I can tell

her anything and I know my secret is safe. She's such a good friend to have, and a good listener too if she's not getting bored, which happens sometimes, but not too much. Anyway, I had to tell her today about what is going on with Megan because I am totally confused. What is going on??????

Tonight Megan called me. It was great, I guess. I was on the phone with my other friend Derek and she called. We talked for over an hour about *EVERYTHING*! One topic that happened to come up was the semiformal and what she said got me really confused. The subject of the semi came up and I asked if she was going and she said she was going with herself, and then she told me I should ask Jessica! So does that mean that Jessica likes me or does it just mean that Megan doesn't like me? *I DON'T KNOW!!!* I can't help myself for liking her because I'm a romantic.

Go ahead and shoot me then.

Billy

12-1

Okay, so it is a brand-new month and now football is over and the first thing I have to say is that *I BROKE UP WITH BLAIR D.* and I am glad. I mean, our breakup has been coming for a while, but I just haven't had the nerve to do it.

I just feel that Blair is an immature little girl who needs to grow up. That is the reason why I dumped her. She was so corny with all her stupid jokes and all her stupid "romantic" ideas and her stupid talk all day is so childish and annoying. The thing that really pushed me over the edge was today by the lockers when she was hanging all over me and wouldn't get off even when I asked her to. She just put on this whiny voice. What just sucks is that I have spent the last two days calming her down after our breakup and I wish she would just get over me already.

Another thing that is stressing me out now that the holidays are over is that I have had two research papers including my history project to finish in the past week. Do I hate those things? Yes—with a passion. When is everything going to slow down? I thought maybe once football ended life would lighten up a little but everything still feels so *HEAVY*. How can I get anything done at all when everything & everyone around me is dragging me down?

Katie

December 1
@ 3:00 P.M.

I'm in photography class right now and I'm running on like 2 hours of sleep—the result of a

10-page history term paper project that had to be done. I'm just a little bit tired but now I'm on my way to chorale and I have to wake up fast. Yesterday was worse than today so I think I'm doing better already. Ugh. I feel terrible though.

Brad tore a ligament in his calf yesterday. Ouch! He made the varsity basketball team at his school but within the first 5 minutes of the first practice he fell and got hurt. My words to him before getting off the phone *just before* the tryouts were, "Promise me you won't get hurt." Oh well . . . I'm happy that he made it anyway. The competition in his school is really rough and he was one of only 2 juniors to make the varsity team. That's the best part of this relationship, sharing in his joys but knowing that the feeling is mutual. It's the first time I've been in a relationship like this. Unlike other people we won't mention. He wanted to see me when he got hurt too, as if that would ease the pain of it all. He's picking me up from school today. It is so hard to go through 6 whole days without seeing each other. But I have to deal with it. It has to be done. I have to be strong!

Every morning, I anchor the morning televised show and my coanchor Alex is the funniest guy I think I have ever met in my life!!! Over the course of the next month Alex says he's going to ask me if I think he's cute, or if I want to go out with him. Of course it's just a joke, but we're going on a mock "date" with a camera crew on Saturday. Here's some of the places where he's taking me:

The meat dept. at the supermarket
An electricity plant
The hospital cafeteria (for dinner)
The puppy store

God knows where else he wants to go—he's a sick, sick child. They're going to air the tapes and it will be soooooo funny. I think everyone in school will get a huge laugh out of the whole thing.

Later @ 12 A.M.

Okay, I am feeling upset right now. When Brad picked me up from school today I got into the car and we were having this normal conversation and then all of a sudden he said, "My grandpa died today." I really had to do a lot to keep myself from getting upset. First of all, I am so tired I can barely stay awake and plus I had a really long couple of days so I am a little edgy. But I held back from crying because he needed me. His parents weren't home to comfort him and I felt so helpless. He had no one to talk to and he wouldn't cry in front of any of his friends. We parked the car until pretty late and he just cried on my shoulder. I had to be strong for him. I will be strong!

my quote for the day from mom):
"We come by love not by finding
a perfect person but by
learning to see an imperfect
person perfectly.
Teresa

Dec 1 (8:25 p.m.)

Dear Diary,

Last night I went to my brother's hockey game and met this girl that he is kind of "with." She lives in a nearby town and she is really awesome! Her name is Tara and we could talk about anything and everything, *TOTALLY!*

Surprisingly she told me she has only hooked up w/1 guy, her ex. I realized that before I met her and talked to her I had seen her in a different way. I judged her as a bitch before I even had a chance to know her. And that is so wrong. Quick story—

There was this time a couple of weeks ago when these stupid girls at this other hockey game started making these comments to me. I was ignoring them and then this one girl yelled, "Yeah, you think you're so hot and you're just not," and she was obviously talking to me b/c I was the only girl standing up there. And yes, we had words, but the main point is that it is really *SHITTY* that people who I don't even know have the right to any kind of opinion about me! And look at *me*—I was no better than they were—there I was doing that whole

144

judging thing on Tara! Anyway, back to the game. Tara and I really clicked and that felt so good. . . .

Also at the game last night there was a guy I noticed on the team who I had never seen before. He has dark hair, a shaved head (kinda), dark eyes, and he is *ABSOLUTELY GORGEOUS*! I asked Tara's sister (who was also at the game and has a boyfriend on the team) who the dark-haired guy was and she said his name is Leonardo Abbruzi. Now that is soooooo Italian. Yummy! AND he's Leonardo *JUST LIKE LEO DICAPRIO* . . . my fave!

Well, me and my mom were walking out of the rink and we saw Leonardo getting into his car. So she yells, "Hey, is that you #24?" and he said, "Yeah," and then we started talking to him and we introduced ourselves to him. My mother is just awesome when it comes to guys. Another short story—

My ex—who I met through my best friend Gina—started talking with me because of my MOM! One night in a Target store I was with my mom and we saw him, but I didn't really realize it was him at first. We ended up in the same aisle as him and his friends and he was smiling at me and I was smiling at him and then I suddenly realized who it was, that it was Gina's pal Rusty and I told my mom. But I wasn't 100% sure yet. So she goes, "Well, what's his name then?" and when I told her she marched over to him and his friends and was like, "Which one of you is Rusty?" So he said he was, and then she said, "So do you know my daughter Teresa Joan?" and he nodded and said he knew about me because of Gina.

I could *NOT* believe my mom actually did that. Way to go! Well, it ended up that Rusty went home that night, called up Gina, and asked for my number. He was interested, and I was absolutely flipping!

For sure, Mom can work miracles. I should bring her w/me everywhere. It would be so cool if she brought me even *more* luck with Leonardo . . . like a boyfriend/girlfriend thing! Now, *that* would be an amazing X-mas present, right?

Kevin

12/2

Christmas is coming WAHOO!

I told my mom already what I wanted:

Norelco electric shaver (I freakin *hate* having to shave every other day)

Rollerblades (I like to a lot of times)

If I can, a phone (for emergencies) like a portable cell phone for my car—I dunno if I will get a new one b/c she'll prob. just give me her old one and get a new one for herself

Little stuff like gift certificates from stores (like the Gap or Tower or maybe even a few Nintendo games for me and my little sis to share (mostly for Zoe, of course)

That's about it though.

Monday this week was like a huge drag. Like the month is already starting off slow. I am ready for vacation already—*BRING IT ON!* This week feels so long and there are two whole days left.

I had lifeguarding the other day and it was ok, better than I thought it would be. We actually got a few breaks so no one died or anything from like drowning or being tired or whomping their head on the bottom. Mostly the people in the class are really cool. Even the instructor. Oh well, ta ta

p.s. I feel totally sick all of a sudden like I'm gonna puke. I think there's flu going around.

Baxter

December 2

I stayed home from school today. I had a fever and I was throwing up. A very pleasant sight. I've been on the phone already with my friend Derek like 3 times this afternoon. He was trying to help me out with this whole Megan situation. Hey, maybe that's why I can't stop puking.

So he told me that I should not beep Megan until later in the week. There have to be so many days in between beeps or else it will look like I am rushing things and she will get freaked out. Ok whatever. I don't understand why she cannot just pick up the phone and call me. So far I have beeped her at least 100 times this year and she has only called my house once.

Megan did tell me the other day that she liked Cartman on *South Park*. I watch this show all the time it is so so so so so so so so so FUNNY! When she told me that she liked it too, I printed out a picture of him for her and gave it to her. Now I think I need to find something with Cartman on it and get it for her for Christmas. I feel better already.

Katie

December 2
@ 11 P.M.

Brad is feeling a little better than he was feeling the other night, but I don't think his grandpa's death has really hit him yet. He is acting like everything is fine, when I know that inside it really isn't fine. I can always tell these things. School has been normal lately—just really hard. Brad's grandpa's wake is tomorrow, but he can't handle it so he isn't going to go. I feel bad because that means he will have to stay at home all by himself. So he won't have to be alone, I told him I would come over, so he will come pick me up at school and then we'll go to the hospital for my volunteering and then out for dinner just the two of us.

Emma

I am looking at the clock right now. I am on the phone with Cliff and he is making me watch this stupid movie on HBO while I am talking to him on the phone. We do this a lot, watch TV and talk on the phone at the same time together. I don't know why one of us just doesn't go to the other person's house, but we don't, so there.

Anyway, now he's not watching the movie exactly, but he's talking on and on and telling me about his gym class today and how he is going to weight team tomorrow. Now he is complaining about the fact that he needs to get a job. I doubt he will get one in the near future, actually. He applied for one at the supermarket, but because his brother worked there once, but then he got in a lot of trouble, they'll probably stop Cliff from working there too. I wish I could be more supportive, but the truth is he gave in his application like 3 weeks ago and they still haven't called back. I told him to just go apply somewhere else. He's stupid but I love him. Okay, now I am still on the phone but I can hear his friend just came in his room and now Cliff is ignoring me. That really pisses me off when I am trying to have a conversation with him and he isn't listening. Of course, when I start yelling at him, he punches all the buttons on the phone to make me be quiet. Duh! Now he has me on his call waiting. Now

149

he's back only he said he was on the line with this other girl and she is this girl who *I REALLY HATE*. I never met her but I know for a fact that she likes him and he doesn't even see it. It is *SO OBVIOUS*!

This girl *always* IMs Cliff on the computer and she always wants to talk to him on the phone. I can't believe he talks to her! I hate that and I hate her. Okay, I guess I am a little bit jealous. But she gets to see him every day in school and I don't (he goes to Joyce, not JFK) and I dunno. Maybe I am the one who is being stupid. I just wish she were here right now because I would totally go off on her and say like, "Listen bitch, this guy has a girlfriend so you just *BACK OFF*."

Cliff says this girl knows all about me but I dunno if I believe him or not. I will still keep making comments about her in front of him and I don't care if it bothers him at all. Plus I saw her picture and she is really ugly and really *FAT*. I'm sorry to say it that way but it is the truth. I guess I will get over it eventually.

♡ Emma-'n-Cliff 4-Ever ♡

I have to get off the phone and try to do a little bit more work. This was a really hard week because I had a lot of tests and quizzes. I think I did well on them though, which makes me happy. Okay, now I really am going to hang up and say goodbye. I am soooo hungry so I think I will go eat my dinner. I love McDonald's Chicken McNuggets!

Emma:
  Spaghetti and meatballs, steak, apple cider, peanut-butter swirl ice cream, and burgers w/onions from the Silverado Diner.

Jake:
  Fries and candy.

Marybeth:
  String beans, brown rice, mashed potatoes, Fig Newtons, and tuna fish.

Teresa:
  Cheese quesadillas, mint chocolate chip ice cream, and anything CHOCOLATE!

Billy:
  Ice-cold Coke, cheeseburgers with extra ketchup, and milk shakes. I love fast food.

151

My Favorite Foods   My Favorite Foods

<u>Baxter:</u>
   Meat loaf, chicken cutlets, garlic bread, funnel cakes,
peaches, corn on the cob, baked ziti, tacos, chicken noodle
soup, rye bread, cucumbers, black olives, and macaroni,
macaroni, macaroni!!!

<u>Katie:</u>
   Turkey, diet Coke, and vanilla ice cream.

<u>Kevin:</u>
   Pizza And Chex Mix

Kevin

12/3

Today is Thursday and it was okay since I had a chem quiz that I thought I would do really bad in because I didn't know one of the answers but then (thank God) someone yelled something and then I got it! I think I did pretty good now. After that I went to swimming and now I am just dealing with the rest of my day. I have been debating what I want to get Adina for Hanukkah (which she celebrates for like 8 days) and I think I'm gonna get her a ring with her birthstone in it. I think I saw one set up that I really like and then I'll engrave somethin in it. Maybe I'll put *"For my little hoochina"* ha ha ha. Jake would laugh at me if I did *that* one (j/k). Peace Out!

Jake

December 3

I got myself a job, and the past few days have been good. Kevin is getting a little better as far as how he is acting around us. The love life still sucks for me but I don't care as much these days. If I get some hookups then I am fine. School has been ok. I have to make up an algebra test and that's about it.

Now for my job. I was really supposed to call for this job last school year but I never got the chance. It is a telemarketing job for Stewart Mortgage Company. All I do is call up people to see if they want to refinance or get a lower rate on their mortgage. I went for the interview yesterday and I was *VERY* nervous, but my boss is so cool and he made it much easier on me and I got the job. It's $7 an hour plus commission. I started today and already got 2 leads. That's when a person has a high interest rate and I find out information on them. Tomorrow I have no work though so I'm going to a DJ party across town with Jonny. I will not be home until after 1:30 A.M. My mom doesn't really know what's up with the party though.

Good night!

Katie

December 4
@ 9:30 A.M.

I'm in English class right now and it's 9:30 in the morning and Brad's at his grandpa's burial. I know he is really upset and is probably crying. As I look up at the clock here in class and think about where he is, my head hurts. I mean it really feels like someone is squeezing it. It's never been like this before. I can't stand the thought of him being so upset. He has had such an awful week.

On Monday, after he trained all summer with hopes of making the basketball team, he ended up with a torn knee. Apparently he's going to be out for 4 weeks and he has a brace on him that goes from his hip to his ankle. I know he's in pain but he just won't admit it. He is still worried somehow about what I am feeling over what he is feeling.

We were supposed to go see a musical tonight in the city and I told him on Tuesday (when he found out about his grandfather) that I would cancel the tickets and get another date for us to go, but he refused. He said that after all he has gone through today, he wanted to spend the evening with me so he could be distracted. So we're going to go even though it's the same day his grandpa is being buried.

Later @ 1:00 AM

I just got back from our date and we had such a wonderful time together. Brad really wanted a distraction and I think this time was perfect. Let's see, we went into the city early and there was this booth you could go into to get pictures taken with Santa. Brad was saying no way would he ever get onto Santa's lap (I knew though that he secretly wanted to!). He doesn't have the best sense of direction, so we had to go on my own instincts and directions which are usually pretty right, and we found a place to eat dinner. Brad refused to let me pay—I hate him for always doing that! After we saw *The Sound of Music* we just walked around arm in arm. I am always so happy when I am with Brad, I can't contain myself. I love having someone around me who cares regardless of what happens.

When we were walking together tonight I looked up into his big green eyes and felt his hand wrapped in mine and I thought how lucky we were to have found each other. When they say love comes when you least expect it, I know they're right. It was such a fluke thing that Brad ended up at Gwen's house down by the beach over the summer, and I almost didn't even go—imagine if I hadn't!

Billy

12-5

I am already counting the days until our winter vacation. I miss the warm weather. Vacation and spring—all that can't get here fast enough.

I am ready to crash today. I slept like 8 hours last night but I didn't go to sleep until 4 AM. I'm schizophrenic like that. I am like 2 different people every weekend. It has to be the atmosphere. In school I am more reserved but on the weekend I go *CRAZY*, I have to be doing something wild all the time. It's addictive. I do have to wake up tomorrow at like 6 AM or something to print out my two papers which pisses me off. I still haven't turned those in. Sometimes I just feel like I am the weirdest guy in our whole grade. Yeah, that's me, all right.

Now I have officially started my *QUEST FOR A BETTER BODY*. I have been running and working out every day now. It's for the ladies, of course, my personal health and lacrosse, which I am patiently waiting for to begin this spring. It will be great, actually I am on the team with Jake and we're already talking it up. Hopefully by the end of this year I will be regional champ—and really good-looking. Anything but football! Later.

Teresa

Dec 5 (11:45 p.m.)

Dear Diary,

Tonite I went to my brother's hockey game—going to his games is becoming my life! They were playing @ this super complex in the city against Whittier, this other local college. Even though they lost 10 to 4, I still enjoyed going because I love watching all those guys in action! Anyway, I saw Leonardo and while I was walking into the parking lot, I heard, "Ahem." So I turned around & he was there & he waved goodbye to me! I was *so* excited!

In another part of life, things w/Zach are *LIKE A ROLLER COASTER*. One day he's *so* sweet & things are awesome, then the next day he's a total ass. We were supposed to hang out last night, but he went to the mall w/his friend. He asked me to go but I said no. I told him to call me when he got home. So he called me @ 9:30, but I had fallen asleep. I talked to him, but I didn't feel good & I didn't feel like going out. Then he got all pissed off. That got me sooooo mad because we were supposed to hang out that time and he never called me back & ended up hanging with his ex. Who is HE to get mad at ME? I can't figure anything out. What am I supposed to be doing?

Okay, so then he beeped me at like 3 in the morning with a bunch of 143's (143 means I love you) and 411's (411 means important or call me right away) and I am thinking what the hell? *WHAT IS THAT ALL ABOUT?* He is soooo confusing. It's been about a month that we've been talking and I don't think I can take it anymore.

I was online the other day and I was talking to my brother's best friend Bryan who is in college now but he knows Zach pretty well. Anyway, he was asking me was I with anyone, and I said I was *sorta* w/Zach and he like *FLIPPED OUT!* He's like, don't get me wrong, Zach is cool, but he is *terrible with girls.* He's like I don't think you should talk to him.

Well, I told Bryan that I was still gonna talk to Zach but that I would keep what he said in mind. Now I am even more confused. Okay, it is *definitely* time to do some serious reevaluating.

158

Can you believe this is today's horoscope?

LIBRA Social Life-'n'-Love: Though you often get A's in having a good time, now you're on the honor roll. Sure, there may be a feud with your favorite guy around the full moon of the 5th, but there will be plenty of parties and new cuties around to keep you busy. By the 26th you'll know just who you want to stick with.

Katie

December 5
@ 3:50 P.M.

Nothing too interesting happened today. I spent the entire day at the mall with the girls and accomplished *NOTHING*. Brad and I went back to the mall too tonite and he still would not go near the Santa booth! I saw a bunch of people I knew, including Sherelle's lame ex-boyfriend, who is by the way the *BIGGEST DIRTBAG I KNOW*. Brad couldn't believe the nerve this kid had. Anyway, we left after a while and went to Best Buy and Blockbuster and I *FINALLY* found a Furby! I can't believe I got one either because it is the hottest toy on the market. Patti really wanted one, she will be so happy! I can give it to her for Christmas. It was a lot of money, but it will be worth every penny just to see the look on her face on Christmas morning. My parents were ecstatic when I strolled in tonight with it under my coat—I am the family hero! Brad and I just cuddled for a while tonight and I actually fell asleep on top of him. He makes me feel so safe.

p.s. Tomorrow is 3 months together with Brad! He just left and I miss him already. . . .

Kevin

12/6

Today is Sunday. I miss Adina for some reason I wish she were here right now just sorta snuggling with me or something I can't really explain. I woke up again really late today like 12ish and just chilled for a while because I was a little wiped. Yesterday my whole family got together b/c yesterday was my mom's b-day. So it was Mom, Dad, Joelle, Melissa, Roger, Helene, Neil unfortunately, Zoe, and *OF COURSE* Adina came too. So did my sister's husband and my bro's g/f. Anyway, it was a really nice dinner for her.

After dinner was over, Jake came over for a while and my dad actually pierced his ear and we all hung out. I miss Jake a little. I dunno I think maybe I haven't seen as much of him and the crew as I used to or something b/c so much other stuff has been going on, plus he's always busy too now that he has this new job and all. He is like my best friend—*I LOVE HIM TO DEATH*. If he wasn't here I dunno what I would do. I mean a lot of people even ask us if we're brothers 'cause we are together so much. It's like we're connected and we think alike too. We'll even say the same thing like 3 times in a row when we're together. It is so cool. Sometimes I think it will be so bad to go to college and not see him anymore and I won't have him around every day if I want to.

Today has been a little less exciting if you ask me so I have just been cleaning up shit around the house and spending a little time with my younger sister Zoe. At like 6 tonite I drove over to Adina's and helped her and her family put up a menorah and other stuff for the holidays. I was thinking, when we're talking about Hanukkah, that I would need to get her like 8 or 10 presents or whatever. So I asked her dad and he just kinda laughed at me and said no, that one was prob. fine. That was cool. I love my time with her so much. I wish Jake could find a girl like Adina. I want so much for him to find someone who will love him and be good to him it makes me sick I want it *that* much.

Emma

that he has a new puppy. He is like my best
friend—I LOVE HIM TO DEATH. If he wasn't here I
dunno what I would do. I mean a lot of people even

12/6, 11:12 PM

I am awake but not because I want to be. I am
sick and I can't sleep at all. I have a really bad cold
and I can't breathe through my left nostril. I have
been blowing my nose like every two seconds but it
doesn't make any difference. It is red and it hurts so
much. Everything I eat tastes like nothing because I
can't smell or taste anything. And I can't really take
any of the strong medicine because it makes me like
a zombie. Now I think I am starting to get a
headache. Maybe aspirin will help. Last night when
I was babysitting I used up an entire box of tissues
and I felt so bad about that. I hope I didn't get the
baby sick. Of course normally she doesn't wake up
in the night when I am there, but of course last
night she did. She was screaming and I had to go
and get her. Her big blue eyes were wide open and I
had to walk her around the room for like an hour
before she would shut up and go back to sleep.

Today we are putting up our Christmas tree. It's
a fake one, but who really cares. We used to get a
real one, but my brother would eat all the needles
when they fell on the floor. Yesterday I helped my
dad put up all the lights outside on the house and
the bushes. I think maybe that's how I got sick. We
also have these white reindeers that they put on the
lawn too—they're really cute. I really love

162

Christmas. There are only 19 days left and I haven't really asked for anything special yet, but I think I want to get a beeper.

marybeth

December 6th

> If I could tell the world just one thing, it would be that we're all OK. And not to worry 'cause worry is wasteful and useless in times like these. I won't be made useless. I won't be idle with despair.
>
> —Jewel

words to live by . . .

Oh jeez! I can't believe this but I actually went on Thursday 12/3 to the DMB concert after all and this is the best part I went with . . . *MATT!* He called me up b/c he knew how bad I wanted to go. There was an extra ticket. It was so much fun. I went with Matt and 2 of his other friends. *MATT'S AWESOME!* There was so much weed at the concert—it really reeked. Actually these kids 2 rows in front of us got kicked out for smoking up.

Friday nite I didn't go anywhere. I dunno why though. Probably b/c I was so tired from the concert on Thurs. night. On Sat. morning I had basketball practice at 8:30 AM and after that I had to go see Matt so I could give him the $$ for his ticket. I really want him so I called him up later and asked him if he wanted to hang out and we said maybe we'd go to the driving range, but by the time he got off work and we got there it was closed. So we went back to my house and just watched *Armageddon*. I could see that movie like 500 times. We never hooked up, but we cuddled and flirted and he was here at my place until like 1 in the morning.

So when he took off, I went right on AOL and then he went on when he got home. He said, "I need some sleep so I have to say good night to the love of my life," and I was like yeah yeah, sure sure. So he got all pretend upset and was like okay then 4-get you. So then I told him to read my profile on AOL b/c he is in it. So he looked.

FULL NAME: Marybeth Miller
NICKNAME: MB (that's all and not even that often)
PIERCINGS OR TATTOOS? Ears—yes, but nothing else YET. I wanna get my tongue pierced!
FAVE MUSIC: Anything good
BF/GF/MARITAL STATUS: I've got my eye on someone. . . .
FRIENDS: U guys R the greatest
SIBLINGS: My bro Mitch and sis Kyra
FAVE COLORS: Mellow yellow
FAVE FOOD: I dunno . . . I am not really hungry right now
FAVE DRINK: Water
FAVE SPORT: Basketball and track
FAVE MOVIE: *Dumb & Dumber*

164

CURRENT SCHOOL: John F. Kennedy High
FUTURE SCHOOL: Pleeeeeeeez accept me
DO U HAVE A JOB? It's a very risky job, u don't want to get involved with anyone like me!
ONLINE PIC: Nope nada NO WAY
EVER CONSIDER SUICIDE? WELL> let's not get into that. But I wish you would step back from that ledge my friend. . . .
MTV or VH-1? I still want my MTV even though I love *Behind the Music* and *Pop-Up Video*
COKE OR PEPSI? Yuck! Gimme water (But I do like the Sprite in U too)
IF YOU WERE REINCARNATED AS AN ANIMAL WHAT WOULD U BE? A rottweiler or some puppy . . . something cute and cuddly (hey, don't be a pervert)
DO U HAVE PETS? Uh, that's a negative
WHAT WOULD U CHANGE ABOUT YOURSELF? Quite a bit
WHAT WOULD U NEVER CHANGE ABOUT YOURSELF? My humor and personality
MOST ANNOYING PERSON YOU KNOW: I don't want to hurt n e feelings
BEST CLUB: Clubbing's not my scene
THE MOST OUTGOING FRIEND U HAVE: Sher Bear!
THE LAST THING U DO B-4 U GO TO SLEEP? Talk on phone or online

Anyway, he played dumb after looking at that, and he was like I don't get it and then he said j/k. He said to me that he had his eye on someone too and then he said I gotta go. I told him he should call me tomorrow but he said why would he wanna do that? I said fine then don't, but please do, please do. He just laughed at me.

I want him so much. I think he is like the nicest guy I have ever met.

The thing is that today during the day I think Rick Wright must have been on AOL and seen my profile too b/c he called me up and said, "Who is *THAT* for???" I was like what does it matter to *YOU*? Then he tried to give me this whole guilt trip and I was not amused. *I HATE* that.

Emma

I just opened my e-mailbox and I got this e-mail from Marybeth—

> How r u feeling? ok i figured i would write to you since i have time and i figured it would give you something to read later . . . well, if u happen to talk to matt today, talk to him about me . . . or say how u want me and betsy to come tomorrow so u have someone to talk to . . . b/c i think i am goin with her n e way. then see if u can get outa him what he thinks of me n stuff . . . thanks so much i am surprised that u would do that 4 me seeing that i am such a SELFISH BITCH yeah whatever . . . anyway really i mean it pleez talk to matt 4 me . . . 4 some reason i like him dude but i don't know why maybe b/c he isn't an asshole . . . LOL . . . ok we're rough riders FEEL BETTER bye

I think that is so nice of her to think of me and send me that. Little things like that make me so

166

happy because at least I know she is thinking of me. She said she was a selfish bitch because I guess someone called last night and told her she was one. I think it was that kid Rick Wright but I'm not positive. I wrote her back kind of the same message as she wrote me. She read it but didn't say anything. I am sure she liked it though.

So like she said, I am still really *SICK*. Mom told me I could stay home so I did. I doubt I am going to miss anything anyway. Just a minute ago I called up Cliff and he had to talk fast because he was on his way to go work out at the gym. Things with me and him are going really good. I am trying to think of what to get him for Christmas. I think maybe I will get him a tie and like 2 pairs of sweatpants. He is always complaining about not having anything to sleep in. I just don't want him to think I am being too corny. I have no idea about what he plans to get me but I already told him not to spend a lot of money on me. Plus it's only 2 more months until my birthday and that's right before Valentine's Day so I don't want him to feel like he has to keep getting me stuff. I guess I shouldn't worry about it until the time comes.

Actually I can't believe it's only 2 months until I drive. My parents can't believe it either. I'm just hoping that I'm not too *SCARED* to pass the driving test.

What I'm Afraid Of

Emma:

I have a fear of heights. I can't even climb trees.

I cannot talk in front of an audience.

I never want to say goodbye to my friends because I don't want to lose them.

Marybeth:

The only really, truly scary thing that I'm afraid of is losing someone close to me. Mostly if I have any fear that I think is gonna paralyze or limit me, I will try to overcome it. I have to prove to myself that nothing has to hold me back.

Jake:

I'm afraid of myself dying and of my friends and family dying. I used to be afraid of heights, but then I went bungee jumping and now I love it.

What I'm Afraid Of

Kevin:
  losing A loved one, loneliness, And
silence

Katie:
  Failure
  Spiders
  Being alone in the house

Teresa:
  I have a great fear of rejection
and I don't know why exactly but
I get really insecure about
relationships with boys, and even
my girlfriends.

Billy:
  Getting hurt badly or not having any friends.

Baxter:
  I am most afraid of slipping up at school, where
everything you do counts. And roller coasters, of course.

Baxter

I just got off the phone with Emma and we made a date to go to the mall on Friday because we both have a lot of shopping to do. I don't know what to get anybody but I guess I will figure it out. Christmas is giving me the hardest time.

I finished my homework early today. What a boring day. I had to sit through two periods of my physics teacher talking about the Bohr atom (so it was bohr-ing, ha ha ha!). Then tonight we had to put together all of our confusing notes so he could collect them tomorrow. What a joy. I must say though that I am *REALLY* starting to do well in all my subjects (except math which is so-so). . . .

Dawson's Creek is coming on now so I think I will go and watch it.

Teresa

Dec 9 (9:05 p.m.)

Dear Diary,

I wish my life were as easy it looks on the stupid TV! I am sooooo sick of school for one thing. I really wanna *DROP OUT*! I know a while back I was complaining about my friends (like Stephanie!) spending all their time with their boyfriends and more has happened with that. Gina and the rest of the girls are all going to Wendy's house this week because she wanted to cook us dinner and then we're all gonna catch a movie and sleep over. I think this should be an excellent *BONDING* nite. There are 2 things that you absolutely need to survive high school. Once a month you must have a bonding nite with friends and once a month you also need to just have a relaxing nite on a weekend when you don't go to any parties and you just stay in and rent a movie or something quiet like that. Without those 2 rules I would never survive!

Oh, as far as Zach goes, we're supposedly hanging out this coming Friday nite but *WHO KNOWS*?! I'll believe that when it happens. I doubt it will though.

Jake

December 9

Well, I am listening to the radio and me and Claudia's old song just came on and I realize that I really do miss her a lot. But she is bad for me I guess.

Work is going pretty good. I have been getting a few leads every night so it isn't bad but I want to get at least 5 leads tonite so I get a $20 bonus. The people there are awesome. I'm also trying to keep up with my homework and get good grades. So far so good.

Lifeguarding is going good. My lifeguard teacher is sooo hot. I can't wait until she puts on a bathing suit and gets in the water with us. *HA HA.*

Let's see what else has been going on. This past weekend I DJed a party with Jonny on Friday and drank vodka before we went so we would have fun. There were a lot of hot girls there. This one girl wanted me and Jonny, and she was cute I guess. This new kid that just came to our school was also there and he is really cool. He is Puerto Rican like me, plus he likes raves which is something else I love. The only thing is, he was asking about my car when I told him I had one (even though I'm not 17 and can't drive), and that got me so sad inside because the car I have is my dad's car. I didn't want to tell him that my dad has this disease and can't drive or walk anymore.

Oh, this Saturday past I got my ear pierced by Kevin's dad and that was cool because we spent some time together. But then of course Adina came over and *I WAS READY TO PUKE* because all they were doing was looking at each other and hugging and kissing and I left to go home.

Kevin

This week was so stressed. I had like 2 tests on Thursday and a swim meet that made me really nervous. I wasn't really in a good mood, so I kinda wanted everyone to just stay away from me. Of course I ended up messing up my chemistry test too so I made up 4 or 5 of the answers like fake ratios and a lot of DKs for Don't Know. The history test wasn't as bad. The only good thing about the day was the meet because my adrenaline must have been going crazy. Our team won like 110 points to 54 for the other team. I was in a 200-yd relay where everyone does 50 yds each and we got *FIRST PLACE* in that which was cool.

I also went this week to get Adina's presents (I got her that ring and then a hat too) and that's it. The two of us hung out tonite until like 1:30. She was kinda tired and complaining a little bit so I came home. Actually it's weird because we kinda got into this whole thing about her not trusting me for some reason, so I couldn't deal with that either. Whatever, it will be better tomorrow—I know it will be cuz after all shit just happens. Which makes me think of like one of the best sayings ever from some xtreme sports ad I saw: *"To be old and wise you must first be young and stupid."* ha ha.

ta ta

Katie

I am the luckiest person. For our 3-month anniversary Brad got me a dozen roses again. He has gotten me roses for EVERYTHING—it's amazing. Wow.

Last night I went to school for the sports awards and when I came in it was late and everyone on the tennis team was already onstage! Mr. Marcus the principal totally embarrassed me in front of everyone and then they turned around and started clapping but luckily I was able to get up there without making too much of a fool of myself. Mr. M. said in front of like 400 people, "Anyone who knows Katie understands. And I am sure *everyone* here knows Katie." I guess that's true.

When I was up onstage I was looking around the auditorium and I was noticing the way everyone was dressed. Half of the girls I saw sitting out there look like they didn't care what kind of an impression they made. They were wearing really tight pants and midriff shirts. I suppose it's just to attract guys, but what kind of guys are you attracting when you dress like that? Brad and his friends make fun of girls like "The Mix" who dress in low-cut shirts and stuff. They say they could never do anything with those kind of girls. They say brains are more important.

I think if you present yourself with class, you attract guys with class.

Like Sherelle. She used to dress in really tight

clothes like that. She's a little bit better now though. She also used to date that creep that I saw the other day. He is such a loser. He was practically bragging about the fact that he was suspended from school. He's only a sophomore and he gets kicked out like every month. I don't know how Sherelle tolerated it. But then again, I tolerated Robert, so I can't talk.

Lately it's like I've been seeing through people, and no one seems real to me—there are so many fake people around me—ugh! I guess being fake is a natural part of growing up, before you know yourself. But who knows. I suppose even I can be fake if I have to. We all are. Maybe that's why people dress differently or do stupid things like Sherelle's ex. The difference between being real and fake is when you are doing stuff for you and not for other people. But it's hard to get there.

Slowly I feel like life is pulling me out of this little shell and making me grow up. I see how much it can hurt, but I'm becoming a realer person. I am starting to understand myself a lot better. Being depressed, being betrayed by my friends, and going through that whole Robert thing last year maybe was the best thing that could have happened to me.

Everything is so different as a junior. We're getting older and it just feels scarier than I expected.

Like what's going to happen *now*?

Check out this sneak preview from

Diary of a
Junior Year

volume 3

Kevin

I thought things w/me and Adina were going good but now I think maybe something is up. Here's the deal, when I'm w/Adina I'm psyched but when she isn't around I *DON'T* know, I feel like I *DON'T* miss her a lot and stuff like that. It's weird. It's like I can't make up my mind on what I feel. I've been thinking maybe I'm crushing on someone else, my friend Cristina. It's like I have soooo much in common w/her and I'm never bored around her and there's always something to say. I enjoy times w/Cristina but I *DON'T* want to ruin the friendship we have by making more of it. With Adina, it's just that we *DON'T* have that much in common and she doesn't really talk a lot. I do all the talking. *I wish I could figure everything out w/my love life!* When I think I know what I want, I realize that I *DON'T* want it. I honestly wonder how long me and Adina are gonna last. I can't say. I *DON'T* wanna hurt her and I do care but obviously things just aren't working anymore. I obviously have changed if I am having feelings for this *OTHER* person.

STOP THINKING ABOUT IT NOW. Okay that didn't work ha ha.

Anyway, one more thing that was funny today was when Lazlo was in Math class he was wearing shades b/c he was so dog tired from that Starlight

Christmas shindig last nite in the city. He looked pretty phat but the teachers were like, "Take off the glasses, Mickey." Ha! Ha! Anyway, later on he was *HURTING* in a major way at the swim meet. How do you get a walking zombie to compete in a swim race? The coach was PO'ed. Lazlo bailed on the race and so we lost b/c he is one of the best swimmers. Coach was happy w/my performance though. I am more determined than ever to swim the 100 yd. Freestyle and break the record, since I am only like 4 seconds off. Only 4 seconds! Breaking a record would be the coolest thing ever.

Emma

12/18, 4:48 PM

Get this! Katie went to the Starlight Christmas Concert with her boyfriend Brad! I didn't know she went! This sucks! Major, major gossip.

So here's why it's not cool *AT ALL*. Someone told me this and it's a little messed up because the last time I talked to Katie about it she said her Mom couldn't get any tickets for any of us, *including her*. For the past two years a whole group of us have gone together, but this year when all our parents tried to get tickets, no one could get through, except Katie who said she had gotten us tickets. Okay then we were all really psyched! But a few days later she said she didn't have them anymore all of a sudden and we all thought that was a little weird, but whatever. Truthfully, the person who was most upset by it was Sherelle, because Katie was like her only chance at getting tickets. Marybeth got hers at the last minute through one of her cousins. I don't know. I don't want to make a big deal out of it, but I think Sherelle might say something. Like I am over it. I don't care that I didn't go because I went 2x already and the more important thing is that my sister Lynne went (her friend got her a ticket and she wanted really badly to see *NSync). So she told me all about it. But Sherelle is another story. Whatever.

p.s. Today I have my period and it is just so uncomfortable. Oh well, the only good thing is that now I won't have it on Christmas day.

Katie

December 18
@ 4:15 P.M.

I love being busy at Christmastime! This day has been so jam-packed. From choir to the AMAZING Starlight Concert, I feel like I am ready for anything!

First, we had an all-day field trip with the choir. We went to different schools around town. Then we did a special choir performance at the Senior Center where I actually volunteer sometimes. My choir director said that I have a special way with the people there. I am glad he notices stuff like that in me. I feel so good after performing for them.

The last thing I did today was go with Brad to the Starlight Christmas Concert! Hooray! We just barely made the train at 7:08 and ended up getting there more than a half an hour late, but Brad was okay with that. It reminded me of going *last* year with Robert. Back then, I bought the tickets and paid for parking and everything and all he could do was complain because we were five minutes late. Five minutes! Brad is so much nicer than Robert ever was. Brad never lets me pay for *ANYTHING* (which can sometimes be annoying but we never fight).

The only bad part about today was something I heard through the grapevine. Apparently Sherelle was really mad about the fact that I took Brad to the concert instead of her. She thinks I'm breaking some tradition by not doing it. I know that last year I was the one who got her ticket, but things are just different now. She has no right to expect that from me. Ever since school started she has been totally caught up in her relationship with Bobby and so has Marybeth and neither of them really call me anymore. Why should I go out of my way to please them?

Marybeth

December 18th

Right now I am hysterically crying. I just had a huge blow-up with my brother, who has been *ON MY BACK* all day long and we just finished dinner and I went to go online and I saw that the computer was plugged into his line. I asked really nicely and real quick could I go on and he didn't even answer a yes or a no. So I said "Why do you have to be such a dick about it!" and of course he ignored me. So I said it again and then I said that if he WASN'T such a dick that I wouldn't hate him so much.

This morning was even worse when I asked (really nicely, I might add) if I could borrow a CD. Just one lousy CD! And he said to me in that stupid tone of voice that he gets when he is acting all superior and older than me, he said "I don't think so" and a bunch of other stuff I can't repeat. I was like, Mitch you are such a jerk *ALL THE TIME*, why is that? And I slammed my bedroom door.

I am not talking to him until he apologizes and I mean that.

@ 11:20 PM

Now it's later and I am a little more calm now. I think I am soooo tired and mad from the fight w/Mitch and from baby-sitting earlier today and it just seems like *there is so much to do and so little time to do it*! Oh yeah, I almost forgot the weirdest thing of all that happened to me and Em today. I was talking to Emma and we have noticed this major change in Sherelle lately like she can't be bothered w/us or hang out w/us. Today we only talked for like 1 minute and then she said she had to take a shower. Huh? I prob. won't talk to her now until Monday in school. No joke. I can't believe that we aren't even talking about hanging tomorrow on Saturday. Funny how things change so fast, right? Today was a really depressing day as far as relationships go.

real teens

Diary of a Junior Year

real feelings.
real issues.
real life.

The school year
continues, and
so does the drama.
Don't miss out.

real teens: volume three

Teen

Coming in October